COOKING WITH STONES

*Ideas and Recipes from
Stones Restaurant in Avebury*

Cooking with *stones*? Listen to a story.

Have you ever been out by yourself late at night, wondering where you would be able to find something to eat? Rain beating against your car windshield; or perhaps with a pack on your back, your feet bruised and your clothes sodden? Our story concerns someone in just such a predicament, afoot on a wet and windy night. Of course, this happened long ago, so it was to be expected that there were few hostelries or habitations along the route. It was also quite natural for the traveller to knock at the door of the first house he came to, stranger though he was.

'Have you got anything spare to eat?' enquired the man. 'No', said the woman at the door. 'I haven't even enough to make a proper meal for myself'. 'Never mind', replied the man, who had spied a pot of water steaming over the fire at the back of the house. 'Please let me in for a little shelter from this rain'. So she did.

The man went to the fire, and sat down to dry himself out. After a bit, feeling warmer but still hungry, he said 'Let me make some soup'. 'How can you make soup, when I have a bare larder?' retorted the woman. 'Ah', said the man. 'I will make you my favourite: stone soup'.

And at this, he drew from his pocket a rounded, blue-grey pebble. The woman looked on in disbelief as he dropped the stone into the water boiling in the pot, stirred it with the big wooden spoon

already resting there, and tasted his creation. 'Mmm', he said. 'This is going to be good soup. But it needs a little something to make it just right. Pass me those leaves', he said, looking at some old cabbage leaves by the door. He stirred them in, and tasted the soup. He frowned, and looked around again. In went an onion hanging from a beam, some dried herbs from a bunch in a corner, a drop of milk from the jug on the table by the bed. He even went back out into the rain, and returned with some weeds, which he added to the pot. 'My, this is really going to be a good soup', he said. 'All it needs now is a little thickening. Have you got any flour?' The woman looked in lots of jars, removing the lids one after another, until she found one with a little flour in the bottom. That went into the pot, too.

'Now', said the man. 'Try this'. He poured some of his soup into a bowl for the woman, and into another for himself. Just as his bowl was nearly full, there was a clunk as the stone dropped in. The man took it out, and wiped it clean. 'Don't want to eat this', he said. 'I must save it for another soup'. But the woman was already eating hers, and the look on her face said she was enjoying it. 'Well', she said, as she put her spoon down by the empty bowl. 'I'm so pleased you showed me the recipe for that soup. To think it was made with just a stone'.

Now *that's* cooking with Stones.

© 1989 Stones Print

ISBN 0 9514076 0 0   Cooking with Stones (hbk)

Designed & Produced by Stephen Nelson MCSD

Illustrations by Phil Gleaves (Endpaper re-drawn from an original woodcut by Blair
Hughes-Stanton), Nancy Anderson, Esther Brimage, Clare Stroud, Jessica Jenkins
(including cover), Caroline della Porta, Felicity Roma Bowers, Debi Ani, Sally Renwick,
Tania Lomas & Alison Dexter. Photography by Michael Pitts.

Phototypeset by PCS Typesetting, Frome, Somerset.
Origination by Adroit Photo Litho Limited, Bristol.
Printed by The Westdale Press Limited, Cardiff.
Bound by Quality Print Finishers, Bristol/Richard Harsher Limited, Romsey, Hants.
James Burn, Oxford/James Burn Loose Leaf, Oxford.

CONTENTS

INTRODUCTION

Photographs by Michael Pitts

On St Valentine's Day, 1984, Hilary signed a rental agreement with the Wiltshire Folk Life Society for the ground floor of a former stable block. Two days later, 'The Wiltshire Gazette and Herald' carried a staff advertisement for 'an exciting new fresh food restaurant in Avebury'. This venture was to be called Stones Restaurant.

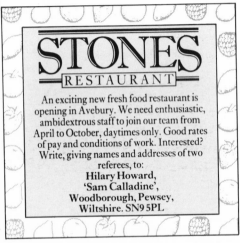

STONES
RESTAURANT

An exciting new fresh food restaurant is opening in Avebury. We need enthusiastic, ambidextrous staff to join our team from April to October, daytimes only. Good rates of pay and conditions of work. Interested? Write, giving names and addresses of two referees, to:
Hilary Howard,
'Sam Calladine',
Woodborough, Pewsey,
Wiltshire. SN9 5PL

Hilary, like me, was an archaeologist. We were both disillusioned with our profession. The long story of past human endeavour is incredibly exciting, but the rigours of academia, bureaucracy and appalling funding were pushing that story ever beyond reach. At the same time, we had become increasingly unimpressed with what we had been offered to eat when our work took us around the country. When in 1983 Hilary finished her PhD with little prospect of a job, the opportunity to open a restaurant and tackle some of our culinary complaints in practice, was more than she could resist. Coincidentally, I was made redundant a few days before Stones opened its doors.

That these doors did open was thanks, amongst others, to a bank manager (Glyn Roberts, of Lloyds in Swindon) and a father in law (Roger Pitts) who were sufficiently caught up in Hilary's enthusiasm to offer the required loans, overdrafts and guarantees. There were doubters, and they could perhaps be forgiven. Hilary's only knowledge of professional catering consisted of harrowing memories, as a sixteen year old girl, of trying to serve processed peas with silver spoon and fork at a tea room in Yorkshire!

In the five years since the first opening, Stones has gone from strength to strength, and is now almost as well known as the ancient megaliths from which it takes its name. Over

a hundred staff (several of whom have stuck with the restaurant through more than one season, one key team member – Rachel Smith – having reached Stones through that original job advert) have cooked, cleared and washed up for a quarter of a million customers. Despite the size of the operation, the approach is still more akin to someone preparing a meal for a group of friends than it is to 'mass commercial catering', albeit on a grander scale, whether it's the flour by the tonne, the weekly thousand eggs or the £2000 plus monthly fruit and vegetable bills (not to mention the VAT returns ...).

The page opposite was written in 1989. A lot has happened since. Our team continues to strengthen, and grow in experience (not to mention, for some, in height!). Which is just as well, as the amount of food we have to make grows apace; it is now quite normal for us to welcome over a thousand people a day. We have built a new kitchen, and improved facilities for our guests. We have found new food suppliers – the most significant being Prestberries Organic Foods, for most of our fruit and vegetables. We have a new ale: Bunce's, from Netheravon (near Stonehenge) is a fine beer from a tiny brewery. And we now have equally fine organic bottled beers, something unheard of when we first opened.

Inevitably, not all the news is good. There has been a succession of nation-wide "food scares" which, though well intentioned at heart, has in some respects left the consumer less well off. Take cheese. The award-winning Castle Hill cheese, referred to in the "Cheese & Ale . . ." chapter, has gone: the owners could not afford recommended changes to old farm buildings. Neither is there any unpasteurised Stilton – a momentous loss to English culture.

To fully reflect all the changes would need a new book. In the meantime, this – slightly amended (thanks Liz and Esther) – Cooking with Stones is still exciting, innovating and all the other nice things that have been said of it. Happy cooking!

Michael Pitts
Green Street, Avebury
Autumn 1991

HEARTFELT THANKS

Eating is a social activity, and a restaurant is fundamentally about people as much as food. A restaurant is also extremely hard work! When you have been going 15 hours a day for weeks without a break, and someone offers to work on their days off (without being asked); or when a customer writes in to thank everyone for the experience they had at Stones; or when an engineer abandons a weeekend with his family to wrestle with a particularly fractious piece of equipment: at times like these, you know you have friends, and the world's on its proper axis. Without many, many friends, there would be no restaurant, and no cookbook. Thank you, everyone!

Amongst the more than a hundred workers at Stones over the past five years, we would particularly like to thank: Vanessa Brunning, Simon Burgess, Claire Compton, Paul Compton, Debra Hewer, Carol Hinchcliffe, Isabel Mumford, Jayne Napier, Mark Randerson, Esther Smith, Rachel Smith, Kit Stead, Martin Trott and John Wilding. Most of the sweet baking recipes were tested for the book by Claire, the sponges by Esther and something somewhere was tested by Rachel. Noah's Rainbow Pie is Rebecca Howard's.

Christopher Lewis, our potter, astonished us in 1984 by being the only non-food supplier to deliver on time, and he had to make his goods himself! Chris still makes all our crockery, at his pottery near Newhaven in East Sussex, now with his assistant Tony Dasent. The Stones logo is the work of the same person who produced and designed this book for us: thank you, Stephen Nelson.

9

Most of our favourite food suppliers and growers appear elsewhere in the book, so it remains here only to single out Steve Perry and our other friends at Nova Wholefoods, Bristol; Kate Freeman of The Wayside Shop, Etchilhampton (organic produce); Helen and Kate Hobsley, Bishopstone, who have recently come on tap with superb organic vegetables and herbs from their own (rented) farm; Bernie Smart and the Smithers brothers who have supplied us from Covent Garden; and Church Farm Dairy, Marlborough. We wish we had discovered Roundstone Catering Services earlier: as soon as something melts, floods or disintegrates (most pieces of equipment attempt at least two of these) Roundstone are there.

They don't receive many bouquets, so it is pleasant to be able to thank some of our media friends. On the 'Wiltshire Gazette', Nigel Kerton (not a bad journalist, even if he does eat meat!) and Brian Woolley; 'Caterer and Hotelkeeper's Nigel Gardner, who wrote such a sympathetic feature on us; at GWR (our local commercial radio station), Simon Cooper and Fiona McDiarmid; and at BBC Pebble Mill (Radio 4), Lucy Lunt and Marjorie Lofthouse, producer and presenter respectively of our 'Radio Times Enterprise Award' programme broadcast in August 1988. It is no exaggeration to say that without the supportive interest of people like these, we would never have had the courage to take on a project as risky as this book. We owe a lot to you.

Last and first. Penelope and Rosemary Ellis, regular customers still, were the first to come through Stones' doors. Thank you, and thank you everyone else who keeps coming back. This is your book; it is also your restaurant.

RECIPE NOTES

All vegetables, fruit and eggs used in the recipes are medium sized unless otherwise stated.

The baking temperatures (in celsius) and times given are for a convection oven. If you have a static oven, you may have to increase the temperatures by 10-20° and increase the baking times slightly.

As to equipment, you probably will have everything you need already in your kitchen: sharp knives (use carbon steel), knife sharpeners, solid and heavy chopping board, grater for cheese and vegetables (or use the grating disc on a food processor), zester for lemons etc, brushes for oil and egg glaze, spatulas, accurate scales, balloon and/or rotary whisk, sieve and colander, measuring jugs, measuring spoons, potato masher, nutmeg grater, pestle and mortar, pepper grinder, melon baller, salad spinner, rolling pin, lots of wooden spoons, mixing bowls, garlic press, spare garlic press (if yours break as often as ours do!), cooling wires for cakes, heavy based saucepans with well fitting lids, a wok (for stir frying), cake tins, cutters for scones, biscuits and ginger people, and lots of attractive ovenproof baking dishes.

A food processor is essential for a few of the recipes (eg «pesto» and «French bean and pecan pate»). A blender will do for mayonnaise and pureeing soups, but a processor has so many uses and will save so much time that it is well worth the investment. Use your processor for pastry and cake making, for grating cheese, and also vegetables for salads and for fine chopping of onions, carrots and parsley for savouries and sauces.

« » These symbols (eg as in «pesto») indicate a reference to a recipe which can be found elsewhere in the book, if necessary via the index of recipes (page 178 ff).

FOUNDATION STONES

Illustrations by Nancy Anderson

Approach our doors any day at noon, and you will be greeted by a symphony of wonderful aromas as Stones' lunchtime dishes emerge from our ovens and pans, and are brought steaming hot to the serving counter. We always have two different savoury dishes (our Megaliths) and at least two Stonesoups. These are complemented by lots of quiches, light savouries, and five sparkling salads. Our rich variety of cakes, biscuits and desserts is a delight to the eye and palate all day long.

Aside from the sweet baking and some of our most popular quiches, our dishes are constantly changing. We hardly ever repeat anything, and no day goes by without someone creating something new and exciting.

As with the traveller in the 'stone soup' story, the prime inspiration for all our food comes from our ingredients. We look to see what flavoursome fruits and vegetables have been delivered that day, what fresh herbs are growing in our garden, which handmade cheeses we have available … and then we decide what dishes to make that will do justice to these ingredients and yet complement each other in flavour, colour and texture.

Further creative inspiration comes from our travels. Wherever we go in Britain or further afield, we seek out local produce and sample the traditionally cooked foods of the region. This gives us a wealth of ideas to draw on when devising new dishes.

The constantly changing British climate is another factor determining what we make on any particular day. Crisp, frosty autumn days cry out for soups rich with ale and robust red wines, hearty bourguignonne casseroles and hot pots. Dreary, rainy days deserve cheering with brightly coloured bakes and stir fries. Hot, languid days are perfect for ice cold soups,

mouthwatering quiches and the lightest summery vegetable gratins.

The dishes described in this book are just a fraction of those which have appeared on our counter over the past five years. They exemplify our range and style of cooking, and we hope will inspire you to invent and create as we do every day. In this introductory chapter, we pass on some ideas and informations from our kitchen, intended to help you both with the recipes, and in your ventures beyond.

SEASONINGS

Crucial to all cooking! Early in 1984, we removed all salt and pepper pots from our tables and hid them under the counter. We were horrified to see so many people indiscriminately scatter these particular condiments over their food without first taking so much as a mouthful. Now, when asked for salt and pepper, we will provide, but always request that the dishes are tasted first. We put a great deal of love into perfect seasonings!

Here we tell you something about the seasoning ingredients and groups of ingredients you will encounter in the recipes. In addition, you should always keep the following four basic seasonings on hand in your kitchen: tamari (naturally fermented soya sauce), lemon juice, sea salt and black peppercorns (for grinding). Use these to correct or adjust the flavour of any soup, sauce or savoury dish. Taste and keep tasting as you create!

Spices

In our recipes, we mention both whole and ground spices. Where ground spices are required, it is best to invest in a spice grinder, buy small quantities of whole spices and grind them yourself. Then the flavour is true. Always try to use freshly ground pepper and nutmeg. Whole nutmegs and black peppercorns store well (some were found on the 'Mary Rose' shipwreck and still had an aroma some 400 years on!) and are far superior in flavour.

When using whole spices in dishes such as curries or spiced salads, toss them with the onions and garlic in very hot oil. Stir and sniff until your mustard seeds pop or your onion turns transparent; then start to add your other ingredients.

Never use ground where whole spices are called for, but do experiment with whole crushed spices (use a pestle and mortar for this) in place of ground.

Mix your own spice 'packs'. Raid ethnic cookbooks for the many good recipes available for curry, cajun, Mexican and other mixtures. These are very satisfying to make, and the aroma of the roasting spices will pervade your house. Use your mixtures to season salad oils, mayonnaise, in place of the suggested spices in appropriate savoury recipes, and as basic flavouring for stir fried vegetables, cooked pulses and grains.

In any recipe, vary the quantity of spices used to suit your taste and your chosen range of ingredients.

15

Herbs

Use fresh herbs whenever and wherever possible. For some dishes, dried herbs are an acceptable alternative, but remember to increase the quantities. Fresh herbs are much stronger flavoured than dried (contrary to popular wisdom). Never use dried parsley, mint or chives. The former look and taste like sawdust and the latter like pencil sharpenings. Always use fresh basil for pesto, and always use fresh herbs in mayonnaise. In winter, when few fresh herbs are available, how about trying watercress, mustard and cress or celery leaves?

Try to grow your own herbs if you can. They do not take up much space, and it's fun. Even if you have no garden, a few pots of parsley, chives and marjoram on your window sill will provide welcome additions to winter salads. If you have a garden, experiment with growing some of the pungent flavoured ancient pot herbs which are making a welcome comeback. Look out for salad burnet, good King Henry, rocket, hyssop, lovage and fat hen.

Experiment with different fresh herbs from those suggested in our recipes, and use lots of varied herb combinations to season your salads.

Alcohol

You will see (if you're a regular customer, without much amazement) as you leaf through this book, that we use a wide range of alcohol in our cooking. Wines, fortified wines, ales, ciders, cognac and liqueurs each impart their own distinctive brand of oomph!

Cook tiny button mushrooms in sherry with ginger for a unique quiche filling; make onion soup luxurious with a generous dash of cognac; simmer brown lentils in dry cider for an extra special pasta sauce; use cider again with leeks, apples and perhaps clotted cream for west country pies; enrich winter soups and casseroles with distinctive strong ales.

Only full-bodied red wines will do in recipes with a bourguignonne flavour, whilst light clarets evoke the atmosphere of Provence. Try creating summer pasta sauces with vino verdi, frascati, soave or moscato; or team new season's vegetables with a delectable mushroom sauce flavoured with a light, flowery French country wine. English country wines can add just the right touch to puddings and desserts.

Whenever you use alcohol in your cooking, remember quality. However good your creative abilities as a cook, and however good the rest of the ingredients, the finished dish will suffer (and so will your guests) if you resort to inferior (heaven forbid) cooking quality alcohol. Follow our example, and never cook with something you would not happily drink!

Vinegars

Our basic vinegars are white wine, red wine and cider. Their main use is in salad dressings, but vinegars are also essential to certain soups, sweet and sour sauces and bakes. Use them to cut the sweetness of fruit and tomato based sauces, to spike or correct soups and for a wide variety of mayonnaise dressings.

Try steeping lots of peeled and crushed garlic, chopped fresh herbs, or bruised summer and autumn berries in a little oil, and then adding to a few pints of chosen vinegar. Bottle and store for a few weeks to create new vinegar experiences.

Preparations

Here we include the mustards, jellies, chutnies, horseradish, tahini and nut butters we use for enriching and enlivening savoury dishes and soups.

Hunt out old and unusual recipes and make as many of these preparations as you can yourself. Aside from saving you money, jelly and pickle making is a satisfying, interesting hobby in its own right. We manage to make all the fruit chutney served in the restaurant (with «savoury rolls», «egghogs» and Mason's lunches), and obtain most of our other preparations from an excellent local supplier – Wiltshire Tracklements.

Thanks to Wiltshire Tracklements, we have been able to experiment with a wide range of jellies and mustards. Try tarragon

mustard, Taunton cider mustard or Devizes beer mustard (made with Wadworth's 'Farmer's Glory') in any of our recipes calling for full strength English mustard. Create salad dressings and cold sauces with fruit jellies, oil and lemon juice. Stir a little apple and herb jelly or mango chutney into mayonnaise for a perfect dressing for potato salad. Try adding creamed horseradish to tomato based casseroles for a spicy winter flavour.

Like herbs and spices, preparations should be purchased in small quantities, and once opened, used quickly, otherwise the flavours will deteriorate. If you cannot find these Tracklements (and they are widely available), delicatessens and traditonal grocery stores usually carry a range of good quality preparations. Find unusual ones and experiment for yourself!

17

FRUITS & VEGETABLES

Ideally, pick your produce and use it immediately. This particularly applies to salad leaves, herbs, tomatoes and the quicker cooking vegetables such as spinach, young beans, baby carrots, mangetout peas and sweetcorn. We devote our garden in Avebury to just these vegetables, leaves and herbs, so we can pick them each morning and run (or pedal!) fast to the restaurant with our bounty.

Much of the rest of our produce we obtain from local organic growers and suppliers. Organically grown fruits and vegetables taste so good! Tiny cherry tomatoes enliven salads and kebabs; marron mushrooms with their deep, rich flavour are wonderful teamed with a wide range of summery vegetables; the autumn roots marry together in magnificent crumbles and hot pots; brightly skinned, pinky fleshed Discovery apples combine perfectly with crisp red cabbage in salads and lightly cooked savoury fillings. Lesser known vegetables such as golden courgettes add a special glow to salads, and grated salsify, the vegetable oyster, makes a wonderful topping for creamy bakes.

As far as possible, follow the seasons with your choice of fruits and vegetables. Delight in young spinach leaves, freshly cut from your garden on a June morning; eagerly anticipate the first peas and sweetcorn of the season; hunt for the rarer varieties of apples and pears; be patient and wait to pull your parsnips and pick your brussel sprouts until after the first frosts!

In recent years, an increasingly wide range of exotic produce has appeared in markets and greengrocers. Lemons, oranges, pineapples and bananas have been joined by orange and yellow peppers, kiwi fruits, avocados, mangos, papayas, sweet potatoes and countless more. These also have their seasons, are fun to use, and can inspire lots of new ideas.

18

Wild foods too add a different seasonal dimension to our cooking. If you can find them, substitute field mushrooms for the cultivated varieties in any of our recipies; add hedgerow elderberries and black-berries to apple pies, fruit salads and pud-dings; collect wild nuts for savoury dishes and salads; bruise any summer or autumn berries to flavour stocks and vinegars.

To summarise: always use really fresh, preferably organically grown produce; grow as much as you can yourself; choose fruits and vegetables according to the seasons; when you buy, whether from a roadside stall or a supermarket, always select the best quality.

Finally, a word about preparation. Remember, the shorter the time between removing the fruit or vegetable from its plant and eating it, the better it will taste. Leave the cutting of vegetables as near to cooking time as possible, for as soon as a vegetable is pierced with a knife, it starts to lose its flavour, colour and food value.

Of the temperate vegetables and fruits, only onions and garlic, and thick skinned roots like winter swede or kohlrabi require peeling. Skinning a potato, an apple or a carrot is like tearing the cover from a book: you can still read it, but it looks dejected and much of its character has gone. As to the rest, merely wash quickly, and in the case of leaves, spin in a salad spinner. Roots just need a scrub with a scouring pad (or, in Stones technical jargon, a 'green scratchy thing'!). Look at the shape of your vegetable before you cut, cut in sympathy with that shape, then steam or saute as quickly as possible. Eat and enjoy!

PASTA

Use either fresh, or good quality dried wholewheat pasta. Purchased fresh pasta is a luxury, but it is possible, though time consuming to make your own at home. Pasta machines are available for around £100, and if you are a pasta addict are well worth the investment.

Fresh pasta requires very little cooking. Just bring lots of water to a rolling boil, add a healthy slurp of olive oil, then the pasta, and cook, stirring all the time, for 2-3 minutes, depending on the variety. Strain immediately in a large colander, and toss with your hands under running cold water to prevent further cooking.

At Stones, we use dried lasagne strips (both wholewheat and 'verdi'), macaroni, pasta shells and tagliatelli nests, all made by Euvita. We have tried many manufac-turers over the last five years, and have found Euvita products by far the best, equalling fresh pastas in flavour and cooked texture. Try to find this variety if you can. Steer clear of no-precook lasagne, whoever makes it. It tastes like cardboard.

To cook dried pasta, follow the instruc-tions for fresh, but increase the cooking times and stir often rather than continu-ously. Tagliatelli takes 5-7 minutes, shells 8-10 and lasagne about 15 minutes. Keep tasting a bit, and as soon as it is cooked but still has a bite ('al dente'), strain and rinse as with fresh pasta.

19

PULSES

All pulses when soaked and cooked, will more or less double in weight. However, it is a good idea to cook more than you need for a specific recipe; then you will have some available for salads, soups or quick snack meals.

When cooking pulses, other than lentils, rinse, then soak them (for a day or a night). After soaking, drain and put in a saucepan with lots of hot tap water and a few bay leaves. Put on high heat and boil until tender.

Prepared like this, pulses take a surprisingly short time to cook. Even for the quantities we use in the restaurant, 45-60 minutes boiling is sufficient for the longest cooking (black kidney) bean. Smaller quantities take less time, so forget the oft recommended pressure cooker, and use a pan. As your beans are boiling, taste one occasionally, and as soon as your taster is tender, take immediately off the heat, drain and rinse under cold running water.

There is no need to pre-soak lentils. Specific cooking instructions for red and brown lentils are provided within the recipes in which they are used. If you require brown or green lentils for salads, first rinse, picking through carefully for stones and other foreign bodies (lentils have a bad track record here), then cover with hot tap water and boil until tender. Lentils do not take long, so keep tasting!

Pulses are magic. Other than cooking them, you can also create delicious, fresh, all year round vegetables by sprouting them. Partly because it is difficult to go seriously wrong with them, in the restaurant we sprout mostly mung beans, chick peas, green and brown lentils and aduki beans. Three tablespoons of dried beans will give you 1 or 2 handfuls of sprouts in 2 to 3 days. Mung beans are perhaps the easiest and quickest; adukis can take up to a week before you can use them.

All you need is a large coffee jar, a section of old (but clean!) tights and a rubber band. Soak your chosen bean in a jar of water for 12 hours (say, overnight). Stretch the tights over the jar's mouth and affix with the rubber band. Then pour off the soaking water, and rinse well in fresh tap water (leaving the tights attached all the time). Drain off as much water as you can, and hide the jar in a dark cupboard (use the airing cupboard if your house is cold). Rinse and drain when you get up and before you go to bed, and your beans or lentils will grow into delicious crunchy shoots.

GRAINS

We use long grain Italian or Surinam brown rice for salads and to accompany stir fries. Brown basmati rice is the ideal partner for eastern dishes. Wild rice, once a totally unaffordable luxury, is becoming less expensive, particularly if bought in bulk. It stores well and adds an irresistable panache to risottos, salads and fried rice dishes.

First rinse your chosen rice, then add to lots of boiling water. Simply simmer until it is just tender, then serve plain or tossed with butter, margarine or oil and the seasonings that suit. Alternatively, cool quickly like pasta for use in salads or refried rice dishes. Treat rye and other whole grains in the same way as rice. Keep testing the occasional grain to make sure you DO NOT OVERCOOK!

NUTS & SEEDS

Universal ingredients! At Stones, we use nuts (brazils, cashews, hazels, red- and paleskin peanuts, pistachios, walnuts, chestnuts and pecans) and seeds (sunflower, sesame, pumpkin, pine nuts) throughout our range: from soups through megaliths and salads to baking and puddings.

For savoury use, toasting nuts and seeds really brings out their flavour. Preheat your oven to 200° and spread quantities of the nuts and seeds you require over individual oiled baking sheets. Pop into the oven and toast, turning occasionally until golden brown. You will learn to know when they are done by the toasty, nutty smell escaping from the oven. A healthy pre-oven splash of tamari, or a sprinkle of powdered ginger or Chinese 5 spice can lend new dimensions to toasted nuts and seeds for salads, soups or megalith toppings.

We use pureed toasted nuts with a wide variety of sauteed and stock simmered vegetables to create soups; chopped, toasted peanuts are essential to our various chilli sauces; toasted nuts and seeds add variety to oat-crumb-margarine/oil crumble toppings; and as to desserts, our filled sponges have always been characterised by their distinctive nut toppings.

One particular seed, used in large quantities at Stones, has not yet been mentioned. We use alfalfa seeds only for sprouting. Quicker to sprout and more prolific than any of the pulses, they create an intriguing addition to our green and other leafy salads. Follow the instructions for sprouting in the pulses section and just watch them grow!

21

TOFU

'Religious faith should be like tofu: it is good under any circumstances' (inscription on the wall of a Japanese temple).

This wonderfully versatile ingredient, essentially a soyabean curd, has been manufactured in oriental homes for centuries. Itself virtually tasteless, it readily absorbs the flavours of other ingredients, and so can appear in endless guises. We use fresh firm and smoked tofu at Stones, and both varieties are readily available in natural food shops (in packeted blocks weighing about 10 oz/280 gm).

Fresh tofu should be used as soon as possible after purchase and always stored in the fridge. It is possible to freeze fresh tofu, and this completely changes its texture. Instead of being firm and creamy, it becomes quite dry and chewy and thus imparts a different character to the dishes in which it is used. Smoked tofu need not be refrigerated; but watch the 'sell by' date!

We always press fresh tofu before marinating. This way, it absorbs the marinade better, holds any chosen shape, and is less likely to break up during cooking. To press, simply place the drained tofu onto a wooden board covered with a folded clean tea towel or lots of paper towels. Put another tea towel or more paper on top and cover with a second board. Place a heavy weight on everything and leave for at least an hour. Any excess moisture will have been absorbed by the towels and the tofu will be ready for marinating.

DAIRY & EGGS

Some five miles north of the restaurant and situated on the edge of a very large town, there is a friendly farm with a Guernsey herd. It is from here that we get the rich double cream which accompanies fruit salads, pies and fudge cake. From here also comes our unsalted butter, especially made for us by hand.

Five miles to the east, high up on the Marlborough Downs, is one of the largest free range egg farms in Britain. Martin Pitt, of Levetts Farm, has supplied us with his delicious eggs sinced we opened in 1984.

Every Thursday, Graham Brasier arrives from somewhere in outer Cornwall in a car laden with clotted cream. Once described by Prime Minister Gladstone as 'the food of the gods', this unique west country delicacy is made by gently scalding high fat milk, then quickly cooling it as soon as the characteristic golden crust has formed. There is no real substitute for Cornish clotted cream in a Stones cream tea!

When buying your eggs and dairy products, chose with the same care that we do. Visit local farms or delicatessens, try to find farm made butters, yogurts, cottage cheese, fromage frais, creams and hard and soft cheeses. We are leaving consideration of our hard cheeses, which play such an important role in the restaurant and not least the recipes, for another chapter.

MARGARINES & OILS

'Block for rubbing, tub for creaming'. This enigmatic note used to be fixed to our dairy fridge door as an aide memoire to initiates (and sometimes old hands). It referred to the two margarines in the kitchen and the different processes they are used for.

'Block' refers to the hard, pure vegetable margarine we use in all recipes requiring the 'rubbing in' technique. We buy this margarine (we use Granose's) in 500 gm blocks, which we store in the freezer and always use, chopped, in its frozen state. It 'crumbs' much better this way, and results in a lighter product. There are few substitutes for Granose (it is completely free of animal products and gluten), but you should experience little difficulty in obtaining a supply.

Soft soya margarine comes in 500 gm 'tubs', and lives in the fridge. We use this for all recipes which begin 'cream together ...', except, of course, where butter is called for. Any quality brand of soya margarine is fine, but if for some reason you cannot find it, try using soft sunflower margarine instead. Obviously you should read labelling carefully if you are concerned about particular ingredients or additives.

Our favourite all purpose oil is sunflower. Very light and without a distinctive flavour, we use it for baking and sauteeing, for sauces, in dressings, and for oiling baking sheets and megalith dishes.

Other oils you will encounter in this book are olive, walnut, sesame and coconut. We use only extra virgin olive oil (the first pressing of the olives) for salads and dishes with a mediterranean flavour, and cold pressed sesame and walnut oils for salads and stir fries. Cold pressed oils are worth the extra expense for their deep rich flavour.

Beyond these, oils to try are soya and rapeseed in place of sunflower; groundnut, grapeseed and mustardseed for salads and sauteeing; and toasted sesame oil to add a dash of pure magic to oriental dishes.

SWEETENERS

Light muscovado sugar is an unrefined, fine textured, lightish brown cane sugar. We use this sugar in all our baking based on the 'creaming' method and for certain other recipes where a particularly light texture is required. Do not confuse light muscovado with 'soft light brown sugar', which is a refined product with added colouring.

For folding into 'rubbed in' baking recipes, use unrefined demerara. The third and final sugar in use at Stones is an unrefined granular light cane sugar, usually available as 'golden granulated'. Finer than demerara, but more grainy than muscovado, this is the sugar we offer for sweetening tea and coffee. In the kitchen it is used for mayonnaise and for correcting soups and sauces.

Our organic clear and set honeys come from the Yucatan peninsula of Mexico. Most of our honey disappears into the bread we make each morning, but it is also used in baking, salad dressings and certain soups. Yucatecan clear honey is wonderful with set natural yogurt!

Maple syrup is a delicious alternative to honey, and do try substituting maple syrup for part of the sugar in baking recipes. Molasses is for ginger people! Use apple or blackcurrant fruit concentrates for salad dressings, or fruit puddings and to replace sugar if you are cooking for someone on a sugar free diet.

FLOURS

The principal flour we use at Stones is an organically grown 100% stone ground wholewheat flour from Rushall in the Vale of Pewsey. This is the flour we use in all our baking. It makes wonderful «bread», yet at the same time is light enough for the lightest of sponges.

Doves Farm 'Malthouse' is used exclusively in breadmaking. This is a textured flour made from a blend of wheat, rye and malt flours with added whole grains. 'Stone-white', again from Doves Farm, is a stone ground, unbleached white flour. We use a little of this to 'start' our bread. Because the bran has been sifted out, the gluten (which aids rising) is more concentrated, so the bread rises faster than it

would with all 100% wholewheat and Malthouse. This can be crucial, particularly on Sunday mornings when several giant batches have to be made! For our «basic pastry», we use half Stone-white and half 100% wholewheat. Lots of different people make pastry in the restaurant, and this formula is generally found easier to handle than all wholewheat.

Similar flours to these three can be found nationwide. When looking for your local equivalents, try to find organically grown flours; read the label carefully on the Malthouse type package – many varieties of this type of flour on the market are bleached then coloured; make sure your white flour is unbleached.

All flours differ slightly in flavour, texture and behaviour. Some, for example,

are more absorbent than others and hence require more liquid, whilst some are finer and respond badly to overhandling. Get familiar with the characteristics of the flours you can obtain!

Other than these, our main three flours, we also use brown rice, soya and chickpea flours for our gluten free baking recipes. Soya, chickpea and buckwheat (also gluten free) flours all have distinctive nutty flavours, and make wonderful pancakes. Carob powder, technically a flour, features in many of our rich cakes and desserts, and is also the secret ingredient in our magic bread! All these flours are easily obtainable from natural food stores. Use them, experiment with them, and look out for others. There are more!

CHEESE & ALE...

Illustrations by Esther Brimage

When spending more than a few weeks away from Britain (particularly so if in north America, where the absences are mocked by peculiarly characterless alternatives) one can find oneself missing, indeed craving, three foods and two drinks. The apples, breads and cheeses of Britain are an essential part of our heritage, as are the ales and ciders which accompany them so well.

At the restaurant, we stock one of the country's finest ales (Wadworth's 6X), we enjoy a good variety of organic English apples and ciders and we bake our own bread with local flour. We are especially proud, however, of our cheeses, brought to us from some thirty farms in western England and Wales by Adam Cassels (of 'Fine Grade Cheeses'). Adam, himself a former cheese maker, arrives every fortnight with a van full of – we never quite know what, until the door slides open and we gather round to see and taste what is revealed.

What is so special about most of these cheeses is not just that they have been made on farms, with the farms' own milk (as distinct from creamery factories using bulked milk), rare as that is; nor just the varied shapes and colours; nor their unusual names. In almost every case, these cheeses are made with milk that has not been pasteurised. The distinctive characters of the soils, meadows and animals are allowed to come through to enrich the flavours and aromas of what, in some cases, are arguably amongst the world's finest cheeses.

All but one of Adam's many cheeses (an exceptional cheddar made by a lady in Devon with the milk from her five cows) have gone into dishes prepared at Stones. Over the years, we have come to rely on a few for cooking with,

and these appear in some of the recipes that follow. Of course, you may well not be able to obtain these particular cheeses (just as delights local to you may be unknown to us), so some brief descriptions are given here, to help you to substitute.

If you have never tasted an unpasteurised cheese, you may be forgiven for wondering what the fuss is about, particularly in view of Milk Marketing Board claims to have conducted research indicating that you cannot tell the difference anyway. All we can say, is seek out specialist cheese shops and delicatessens selling real 'live' cheeses, and talk and taste (not forgetting, of course, the opportunities

that Stones offers you). Ignore lables (unless they come from the very farm that made the cheese), which can be misleading. 'Farmhouse', for example, is a name given to a cheese grading scheme devised by the MMB that seems to exclude the great majority of cheeses actually made at farm houses! Furthermore, a cheese with great potential can be made on the farm, but then vacuum packed in rindless blocks so that its real flavour can never develop.

Cheddar A good cheddar has a character so rich that one can be distinguished from another, even in a cooked dish (see «cheese scones»). All the cheddars we use come from Somerset. One of these, Phillip Rainbow's, is a double rarity: traditionally made and matured cheddar using unpasteurised milk, curdled with vegetable rennet (much cheese is made with an enzyme from the lining of a calf's fourth stomach). A wonderful cheddar type cheese that we have recently tasted – but not had at Stones – is from Castle Hill Farm in Sussex.

Teifi Teifi, made by Mrs Peul at Glynhynod Farm, Dyfed, is one of our staples. It is a semi-hard Gouda type, and is an excellent all round cooking cheese, with melting properties similar to mozzarella (we use it for our «masterpizza» and «Welsh hot pot»). As well as plain Teifis, you can buy cheeses flavoured with various herbs, spices and garlic.

Devon Oke This is a matured semi-hard cheese, made at the 'Farmers Weekly' farm at Okehampton, Devon. In its younger (and commoner), milder flavoured state, it is sold under the name of the farm, Curworthy. Devon Oke's creamy tang complements spinach particularly well («lasagne verdi with polpettini»).

Gloucester When we refer to Single or Double Gloucester, we are not thinking of the salty, soapy factory made things that go under these names. There are some real Gloucester cheeses being made, including those of the Martells, who have their own herd of traditional Gloucester cattle. We use mostly Single Gloucester, made by Diana Smart at Old Ley Court. These are cheeses to match subtle flavours, like the fresh thyme in «lentil and Single Gloucester squares».

Blue cheeses There are still very few blue cheeses made in Britain, the old faithful Stilton, of course, being the best known, and obtainable nationally. Of the cheeses coming under the 'Farmhouse' scheme, only Colston Bassett Dairy's Stilton is unpasteurised. We would never use the 'cooking Stilton' beloved of many cheese sellers. Stilton is Stilton, and in its 'cooking' state, deserves only to be thrown out.

Shropshire Blue is Stilton reddened with annatto dye (made from a tropical seed). Blue Cheshire is a cheese made uniquely by the Hutchinson Smiths at Hinton Bank Farm in Shropshire, and in our experience, has more character than most Stiltons. Looking like blue Stilton, but with a very distinctive almost fruity flavour, is Dorset Blue Vinney. This has yet to become a widely available product.

Red Leicester Made by Tuxford and Tebbutt, Red Leicester is a bulked (ie uses milk from a number of different farms) pasteurised cheese, and is bland for eating. For cooking, however, it is an inexpensive and very useful all purpose cheese. Its red colour (annatto again) features well in salads, soups («potato with Red Leicester and cognac») and savoury bakes («celery, cashew and almond roast»).

Caerphilly The Caerphilly made by Duckett at Walnut Tree Farm in Somerset, is a superb cheese for eating, whose mild creamy taste is achieved at no sacrifice of character. It is also a good performer in the kitchen, where its rounded, almost sweet flavour is a perfect complement for almonds («courgettes stuffed with Caerphilly and almonds») and new seasonal vegetables («curried autumn vegetable pie»).

cooking. They are all distinctive in flavour. Wensleydale has a wonderful fresh creamy tang. Pink Cheshire has a crumbly texture and makes a worthy substitute for Devon Oke, and try White Cheshire in place of cheddar in baked dishes (but not in cheese scones!). Lancashire and Staffordshire are quite salty cheeses, and so are good with end of season vegetables or dishes involving a substantial component of cooked pulses or grains. Be especially careful with seasonings with salty cheeses like these!

Whether your cheese is eaten unadulterated with some good fresh bread, or incorporated into a sophisticated hot dish, it needs an accompanying drink that can hold its own. As with our cheeses, so with drinks, we are finding it increasingly easy to obtain the naturally produced beverages that are so important to the restaurant. When you are serving a meal replete with local produce, some perhaps from your own garden, what could be better as accompaniment than local ciders, ales or wines, or non alcoholic drinks such as fruit juices or mineral waters? There is a long way to go yet before we all have a local choice, but new offerings are appearing with regularity. Keep your eyes open!

Perhaps the central drink, both at Stones and on the British scene, is ale. We are fortunate to have one of the country's older, traditional breweries close by in Devizes. Wadworth's solid red brick building dominates the town, just as the aroma of fermenting mash wafting over the market place is a reminder of the importance of the brewery to the local economy. The key role of the Campaign for Real Ale in saving so many of our older

Sharpham Izabella Carroll's Bries, made at Sharpham, near Totnes, Devon, have everything you could wish from a good Brie, in flavour, appearance and texture. We use them in sauces (« Brie and red pepper») and they are good for slicing and layering in savoury bakes («red wine and nut roast with Brie »). We have also enjoyed Pencarreg, an organic (but pasteurised) Brie made by Welsh Organic Foods in Lampeter, Dyfed. When cooking with Brie, use the whole cheese: do not discard the white rind.

Amongst the other cheeses we use, Cheshires (pink and white, from the Applebys' Abbey Farm in Shropshire), Lancashire (the Butlers at Lower Barker Farm) Staffordshire (an organic, vegetarian cheese made by the Deavilles at New House Farm) and Wensleydale (from Donald Rutter at Old Beacon Farm, Cheshire) have been useful for eating and breweries, and in paving the way for new ones, is well known. But good ale has by no means a secure future. The big breweries, aware of the demand but unable to meet it directly (a living ale being too fickle a thing for long storage and transport) are turning devious. Pubs are being redesigned to have that 'local' and 'traditional' feel. Centrally produced beers of little character are given 'local' names, even, sometimes, of a defunct (but local) brewery. Beware, and trust your taste buds.

Just as ales, and particularly those made by the small, independent breweries, have to compete against the effects of massive advertising for lager type beers, so traditional ciders fight for space at the bar with heavily promoted drinks that are made with apples, but have as little in common with real cider as a gassy lager with a dark ale, or a plastic wrapped block cheese with a handmade unpasteurised farm cheddar. It is for us, then, a pleasure to be able to sell ciders made by the Dunkertons from unsprayed traditional cider apples: a pleasure clearly shared by many customers! The Dunkertons make a range of ciders, some blended, some from single apple varieties (such as Breakwells Seedling, Foxwhelp or Yarlington Mill). Along with a perry (made in the same way as cider, but with hard perry pears), these drinks are becoming easier to find outside their Herefordshire home, and of course, there are other people in different parts of the country producing their own special brews. Each has a distinctive and complex flavour. Like cheese or ale, cider is a subject for a whole book to itself!

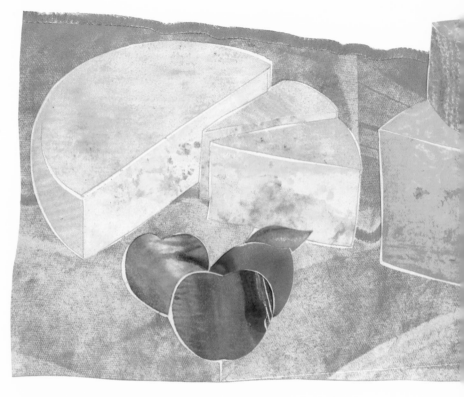

For many, a surprising arrival on the English drinks scene is the grape wine, especially when it is discovered to be very palatable yet distinctively English. We stock a medium dry white from Fonthill in south Wiltshire. Like all English grape wines, this is made from German fruit varieties (specifically, Seyval Blanc, Reichensteiner and Muller-Thurgau), and special procedures are required to overcome the problems of the short growing season. One effect of this is a wine that would not appeal strongly to the drinker concerned about chemical sprays and additives.

In terms of quantity, at least, the strongest future for wines in Britain lies with indigenous plants. At Stones we sell Moniac Wines' meadowsweet (not unlike a Sauterne) and silver birch (similar to Retsina), and Hugh Rock's well known elderflower. There is a wide range of fruits (Nicholas Downs makes a fine dry apple wine in Devon), flowers, roots and other substances that can make excellent wines, and the market is wide open for commercial wineries.

Wild flowers used in wines are grown naturally (Hugh Rock gathers elderflowers in his own organic orchard).

Grapes, outside England as much as in, are another matter. It seems likely that the interest in organic foods will soon be parallelled by a fuller awareness of the artificials floating in even the most praiseworthy wine. The effect on wine sales of a rash of 'E numbers' on bottle labels could be quite dramatic: at present there is no legal compulsion for alcoholic drinks to carry ingredient information. We have recently started to sell organic wines from Italy and France. If you do take care and trouble to avoid chemicals in your foods, you might investigate organic wines. There is already a wide choice available from the right suppliers.

It seemed appropriate to end this chapter with something we do make ourselves at Stones, and in which there has always been great interest: lemonade.

When making lemonade, the first thing to do is make sure your lemons are well washed. Then squeeze the juice from 12 and save both the juice and the skins. Put the skins in a pan, and just cover with cold water. Bring to the boil and simmer for 5 minutes. Take off the heat and strain through a colander into a large bowl. Save everything! When the skins in the colander are cool enough to handle, squeeze what you can from them into the liquid in the bowl. You can now throw them away. Now add the reserved juice and stir in just enough light muscovado sugar to taste. Pour your concentrated lemonade into several large jugs, and refrigerate until ready to serve. For drinking, dilute with about a third water and lots of ice cubes. Add a lemon slice and a sprig of fresh mint to each tall glass.

STONESOUPS

Illustrations by Clare Stroud

According to the mood, preference and hunger of our customers, Stonesoups may be a meal in themselves, or followed or accompanied by a salad or light savoury, or prelude a varied, many coursed meal. Our daily soup duet reflects this range of options. A hearty, richly flavoured chunky soup such as «soupe au pistou» or «mulligatawny» will steam alongside a light or perhaps creamy soup such as «magic mushroom» or «cream of the garden».

When serving soup as a first course, think carefully about the content of the rest of the meal. Consider the colours and textures as well as the flavours in your main course, and select your soup to contrast with, yet complement all these. Try not to repeat any dominant ingredients (mushrooms, tomatoes, strong spices etc), otherwise the meal will be boring. If the main course has a cream or cheesy sauce, choose a dairy free soup. Set off a light main course with a spicy, or rich creamy, or thick chunky soup.

Always follow the seasons in your soup making, choosing the best quality fresh ingredients available. Make the most of garden produce in the summer for light and perhaps chilled soups, and in the colder months raid the store cupboard for lentils and all manner of beans and grains to team with autumn and winter roots.

If possible, make your soup the day before it is required. Cool and refrigerate it overnight, then gently reheat just before serving time. This gives all the flavours a chance to mature and get to know each other better. If you are using milk, cream or cheese in your soup, make the 'body' the day before and add the dairy ingredients while reheating.

For all our stock requirements, for megaliths and sauces as well as soups, we use a vegetable concentrate and find 'Vecon' (available in economical 1 kg jars) produces the best flavour. Unless otherwise stated, the following stock formula has been used throughout this book: 1 tablespoon plus 1 teaspoon vegetable concentrate to 2 pints (1100 ml) hot water. Where miso stock is called for (miso is a fermented soybean paste), or if you fancy using it for a change, substitute 2 tablespoons for the vegetable concentrate.

BRAZILIAN BLACK BEAN

A satisfying supper if served alone with freshly baked bread and a light salad selection. Or a wonderful prelude to a central American meal.

1 onion, chopped
1 clove garlic, crushed
1 large carrot, sliced
2 sticks celery, sliced
2 tablespoons olive oil
small bunch fresh coriander, chopped
pinch ground cumin
1¼ pints (700 ml) vegetable stock
8 oz (225 gm) cooked black kidney
or turtle beans

2 oranges, peeled and segmented
1 teaspoon lemon juice
juice of 1 orange
1 tablespoon dry sherry
1 tablespoon tamari

Saute vegetables in oil with the coriander and cumin. Stir in beans and simmer for 10 minutes with the stock.

Add oranges, juices, sherry and seasonings.

POTATO WITH RED LEICESTER & COGNAC

Sumptuous!

2 large onions, chopped
4 large cloves garlic, crushed
4 potatoes, thinly sliced
2 oz (50 gm) margarine
1 tablespoon sunflower oil
1¾ pints (1 l) vegetable stock
3 sprigs fresh sage

handful fresh parsley
2 tablespoons cognac
2 tablespoons tamari

4 oz (100 gm) Red Leicester cheese, grated

Melt the margarine with the oil, and saute the vegetables on medium heat for 5 minutes, stirring often. Add the stock and the sage, turn down the heat and simmer, covered, until everything is tender.

Remove from heat, cool slightly and puree with the parsley. Stir in the cognac and the tamari and store in a covered container in the fridge overnight.

Reheat gently, and 10 minutes before you are ready to serve, stir in the cheese.

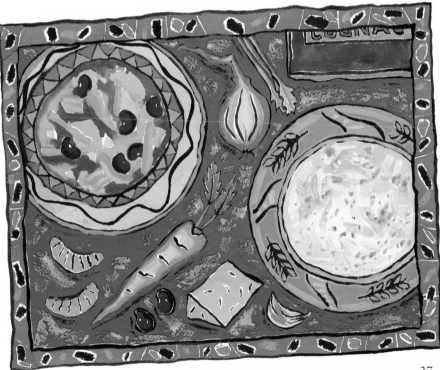

MULLIGATAWNY

This is a wonderful blend of exotic flavours. Everyone loves it (both sides of the counter!), but it's so simple to make.

2 onions, chopped
4 carrots, diced
4 Bramley apples, diced
1 oz (25 gm) margarine
2 tablespoons rhogan josh
½ tablespoon mixed spice
3 tablespoons wholewheat flour
3 pints (1700 ml) vegetable stock
1 tablespoon clear honey
6 tomatoes, sliced
5 oz (150 gm) peanuts
handful raisins

Saute onions, carrots and apples in the margarine. Add spices and flour. Pour in stock. Add remaining ingredients. Simmer for 10 minutes. Cool, and store in fridge for 12 hours.

Puree half the soup, and reheat all in pan.

38

POTATO, LEEK & SHERRY

5 leeks, chopped
knob of margarine
1 lb (450 gm) cooked potatoes
4 fl oz (125 ml) sherry
2 tablespoons wholewheat flour
4 pints (2¼ l) vegetable stock

Saute leeks in margarine until softening. Add potato and sherry, and simmer briefly. Stir in the flour, and pour on the stock. Cool, blend and reheat.

LEEK & BLUE CHESHIRE

6 leeks, sliced
knob of margarine/butter
3 tablespoons wholewheat flour
3 pints (1700 ml) vegetable stock
12 oz (350 gm) Blue Cheshire cheese, grated

Saute leeks in butter until soft. Add flour and stock, and simmer for 5 minutes. Stir in cheese and seasonings.

WELSH ONION

So called because of the Teifi cheese ...

> 7 onions, thinly sliced
> 3 bay leaves
> 1 oz (25 gm) demerara sugar
> 1 oz (25 gm) butter
> 1 teaspoon salt
> ½ pint (300 ml) red wine
> 3 pints (1700 ml) vegetable stock
> 2-3 tablespoons brandy
> Teifi cheese, grated
> croutons

Slowly saute onions, bay leaves and sugar in butter with salt, until the onions caramelise and fall to a soft oniony mass. Add wine, then stock, and remove from heat. Cool, and refrigerate overnight.

Reheat and adjust seasonings. Add brandy. Serve over croutons and a handful of the grated cheese in each bowl.

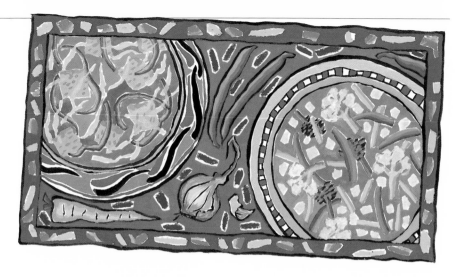

INDONESIAN VEGETABLE

> 1 oz (25 gm) tamarind
> ¼ pint (150 ml) hot water
>
> 1 large onion, finely chopped
> 4 cloves garlic, crushed
> 4 carrots, cut into sticks
> knob of fresh ginger, grated
> 1 teaspoon fenugreek
> 1 teaspoon ground coriander
> 1 teaspoon turmeric
> pinch chilli powder
> ½ teaspoon mustard powder
> ½ teaspoon ground cumin
> 3 tablespoons coconut oil
>
> 1 small cauliflower, broken into bite sized florets
> a few bite sized sprigs broccoli
>
> 4 oz (100 gm) creamed coconut, grated
> 1¾ pints (1 l) vegetable stock
> 10 tender French/runner beans, cut into 2 inch (5 cm) lengths

Soak the tamarind in the water for at least an hour before use.

Saute onion, garlic and carrots with the spices in the coconut oil for 5 minutes on high heat, stirring all the time.

Add the cauliflower and broccoli and stir to coat with the spicy mixture. Lower the heat, strain the tamarind water into the vegetables, and discard the tamarind. Simmer for 10 minutes.

Grate the creamed coconut into the heated stock, and stir until dissolved. Add this to the vegetables, with the beans, and simmer, covered, for about 15 minutes, until all the vegetables are tender.

Cool and refrigerate overnight. Reheat gently the following day, and thin with extra stock if necessary.

39

CREAM OF THE GARDEN

For those of you with a well stocked garden, this recipe should begin 'First pick your herbs and vegetables ...' When served in the restaurant, this soup is a celebration of our own garden inside the stone circle.

2 oz (50 gm) margarine
1 large onion, roughly chopped
4 large cloves garlic, crushed
1 potato, roughly chopped
3 courgettes, sliced
a few bay leaves
1½ pints (850 ml) vegetable stock
zest of 1 lemon
4 oz (100 gm) spinach, washed and roughly chopped
small handful chopped fresh mint
sprig chopped fresh sage
1 tablespoon chopped fresh coriander
7 fl oz (200 ml) single cream

Melt the margarine on gentle heat, and saute the onions, garlic, potato and courgettes with the bay leaves, for 10 minutes. Add the stock and lemon zest, and simmer until all the vegetables are just crisp tender (about 10 minutes). Add the spinach and the herbs, and stir briefly until the leaves are just wilting. Take immediately off the heat, and puree. Cool and refrigerate overnight.

Next day, reheat gently, then add the cream and thin with a little extra stock if necessary.

MUSHROOM & RED WINE

1 head celery, sliced
2 cloves garlic, sliced
2 lb (900 gm) mushrooms
large knob of margarine
½ pint (300 ml) red wine
pinch thyme
pinch marjoram
2 tablespoons tamari
2 tablespoons wholewheat flour
3 pints (1700 ml) vegetable stock

Saute all vegetables in margarine for 10 minutes. Add wine, herbs and tamari and simmer for 15 minutes. Sprinkle over flour and add the stock. Continue to simmer for 20 minutes. Season.

THREE MUSHROOM SOUP WITH RAMEN NOODLES

For this one you need not so much a garden, as a Chinese supermarket.

3 large dried Chinese mushrooms
7 fl oz (200 ml) hot water

knob fresh ginger, grated
3 small cloves garlic, crushed
1 small onion, finely chopped
2 small carrots, cut into thin matchsticks
1 teaspoon Chinese 5 spice
1 tablespoon sunflower oil

7 oz (200 gm) pristine button mushrooms, thinly sliced
1 pint (550 ml) strong miso stock
4 fl oz (100 ml) medium sherry

½ packet buckwheat ramen noodles (discard flavouring sachet!)
4 oz (100 gm) oyster mushrooms, trimmed
1-2 teaspoon oriental sesame oil
tamari
spring onions, sliced for garnish

Soak the dried mushrooms in hot water 12 hours or overnight.

Saute in oil the ginger, garlic, onion and carrot sticks with the spice, on high heat for 2 minutes, stirring all the time. Add the button mushrooms, and stir to seal with the oil. Lower the heat and add the stock and sherry.

Remove the dried mushrooms from the soaking water, and add the liquid to the soup. Slice the soaked mushrooms finely and add these too. Simmer 10 minutes.

Add the ramen noodles and simmer 10 minutes more, stirring occasionally with a fork to separate the noodles. Add the oyster mushrooms, the sesame oil to taste, and season with tamari if necessary. Simmer 1 minute longer, then serve garnished with lots of spring onions.

41

GAZPACHO

The opportunities for sipping an iced soup in the shade of a tree may be commoner in Spain than in Britain. But when the sun does shine and the early evening air is still warm, the evocative flavours of gazpacho can add a touch of magic to an early picnic supper.

> *5 good sized tomatoes*
> *1 fat clove garlic*
> *1 small onion, or some spring onions*
> *1 carrot*
> *1 cucumber*
> *1 green pepper*
> *1 stick celery*
> *½ tablespoon basil*
> *juice of ½ lemon*
> *2 tablespoons olive oil*
> *1 pint (500 ml) vegetable stock*
> *1 pint (500 ml) tomato juice*
> *dash tamari*
> *pepper*

Roughly chop all the vegetables and blend in a food processor in small batches to a chunky puree. Place in a bowl and stir in remaining ingredients. Cool for a minimum of 5 hours. Check seasoning. Serve over ice cubes with garlic croutons. It is extra good with a bowl of cucumber and yogurt.

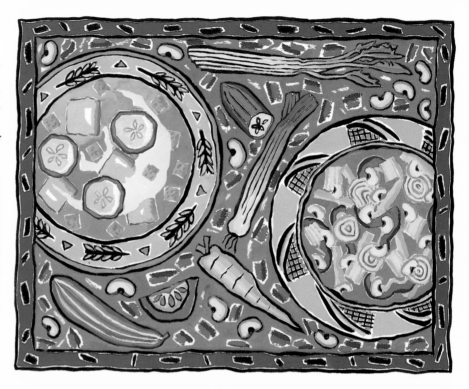

BLACKEYED BEAN & VEGETABLE

A hearty soup for a crisp winter day.

> *1 leek, chopped*
> *1 courgette, sliced*
> *1 green pepper, sliced*
> *2 carrots, sliced*
> *3 celery sticks, chopped*
> *2 tablespoons olive oil*
> *pinch oregano*
> *pinch basil*

> *1 lb (450 gm) cooked blackeyed beans*
> *2 tablespoons tomato paste*
> *4 fl oz (125 ml) red wine*
> *2 tablespoons lemon juice*
> *3 pints (1700 ml) vegetable stock*

Saute all vegetables in oil with herbs.
Add beans, tomato paste, wine, lemon juice and stock. Simmer for 40 minutes.

SOUPE AU PISTOU

Evocative of Southern France, this soup is made special by the addition of freshly made pesto. Smells wonderful as it simmers!

2 large courgettes, sliced
2 large onions, sliced
4 tomatoes, sliced
2 celery sticks, sliced
1 carrot, sliced
2 tablespoons olive oil
2 bay leaves
3 tablespoons «pesto»
2 pints (1100 ml) vegetable stock
handful French beans or cooked haricot beans

Saute all vegetables in oil with bay leaves. Add pesto and vegetable stock, and beans. Simmer for 15 minutes.

CELERY & CASHEW

Simple but subtle.

1 onion, sliced
1 head celery, sliced
knob of butter/margarine
1 bay leaf
12 oz (350 gm) toasted cashew nuts
3 pints (1700 ml) vegetable stock

Saute onion and celery in margarine with bay leaf for 10 minutes. Stir in nuts. Add 2 pints (1100 ml) stock, and simmer for 10 minutes. Cool overnight. Blend, reheat and season, and add more stock if needed.

MAGIC MUSHROOM

Well, that's what several of our customers have called this soup ...

3 onions, chopped
2 oz (50 gm) margarine
1½ lb (700 gm) mushrooms, sliced
2 tablespoons dill weed
2 tablespoons paprika
1 oz (25 gm) wholewheat flour
2 pints (1100 ml) stock
juice of ½ lemon

12 fl oz (375 ml) milk
8 fl oz (250 ml) soured cream

Saute onion in margarine. Add mushrooms and dill and paprika. Stir in flour, then stock and lemon. Simmer for 10 minutes. Cool, and store in fridge.

Reheat following day and stir in milk and soured cream. Check seasoning.

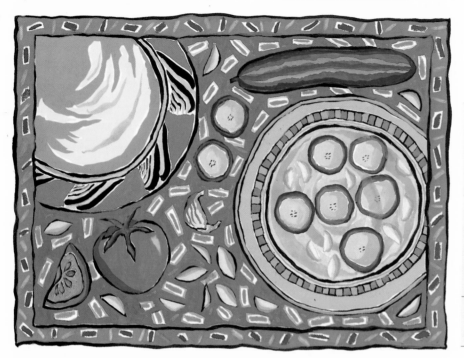

CURRIED COURGETTE & ALMOND

1 large onion, chopped
4 large cloves garlic, crushed
½ teaspoon fenugreek
½ teaspoon cumin seed
1 teaspoon ground coriander
1 teaspoon pickling spice, with chillis removed
1 teaspoon turmeric
½ teaspoon cayenne pepper
2 tablespoons olive oil
6 small courgettes (about 5 inches/12 cm long), sliced
1½ pints (800 ml) vegetable stock

3 oz (75 gm) ground almonds
1 small courgette in paper thin slices
1-2 tablespoons toasted flaked almonds

Saute the onion, garlic and all the spices in the olive oil on high heat for 3 minutes, stirring all the time. Add the courgettes and continue to stir for 1 minute more. Add the stock and turn down the heat. Simmer for 15-20 minutes, until the courgettes are tender. Cool and refrigerate for several hours, or overnight if possible.

An hour or so before serving time, puree the soup with the ground almonds. Reheat gently, check the seasoning, and serve garnished with the sliced raw courgette and flaked almonds.

FRESH TOMATO WITH CREAM CHEESE

This soup can be successfully prepared and eaten on the same day.

1 large onion, roughly chopped
3 large cloves garlic, crushed
1 potato, roughly chopped
2 sticks celery, trimmed and sliced
2 tablespoons sunflower oil

12 ripe tomatoes, pureed
handful fresh dill, coarsely chopped (or 1 tablespoon dried dill)
large pinch ground cloves
1 pint (550 ml) vegetable stock
3 tablespoons cream cheese

Saute the hard vegetables in the oil on gentle heat for 10 minutes, stirring occasionally. Add the tomatoes, dill, cloves and stock, and simmer, covered, on low heat until the potato is thoroughly tender. Puree and season. Return to the pan and reheat.

Stir in the cream cheese just before serving. Serve garnished with snipped fresh dill and garlic croutons.

MUSHROOM & OLD TIMER

There are many 'Olds', from Thumper to Peculiar, and names such as Bishop's Tipple, Winter Warmer or S.O.D. Each of these ales has its own distinctive taste, and any will give your soup that special flavour. Our local strong dark bitter is Wadworth's Old Timer, and it frequently stars at the restaurant in this rich mushroom soup.

2 onions, chopped
2 carrots, chopped
1 clove garlic, crushed
2 sticks celery, chopped
1 bay leaf
knob of margarine
1 lb (450 gm) mushrooms, sliced
1 tablespoon wholewheat flour
1 tablespoon tomato paste
1¾ pints (1 l) vegetable stock
1 bottle (275 ml/about ½ pint) Old Timer ale

Saute onion, carrot, garlic, celery and bay leaf in margarine. As onion softens, stir in mushrooms followed by flour. Cook for 2 minutes, then add tomato paste, stock and ale. Simmer for 15 minutes. Cool overnight. Re-heat, check seasoning, and serve.

45

BUTTER BEAN, CIDER & VEGETABLE

knob of margarine
1 onion, chopped
2 large carrots, sliced
3 celery sticks, sliced
1 parsnip, diced
1 turnip, diced
4 English eating apples, chopped
1½ pints (850 ml) vegetable stock
¾ pint (400 ml) dry cider
small sprig of fresh sage
pepper
8 oz (225 gm) cooked butter beans

handful chopped fresh parsley
5 oz (150 gm) sharp cheese (eg Staffordshire), grated
squeeze of lemon juice

Saute all vegetables and apples. As onion softens, add stock, cider and sage. Season to taste. Simmer until carrots are tender. Add butter beans and cool overnight.

Blend half soup. Return all to pan, and reheat with parsley, cheese and lemon juice.

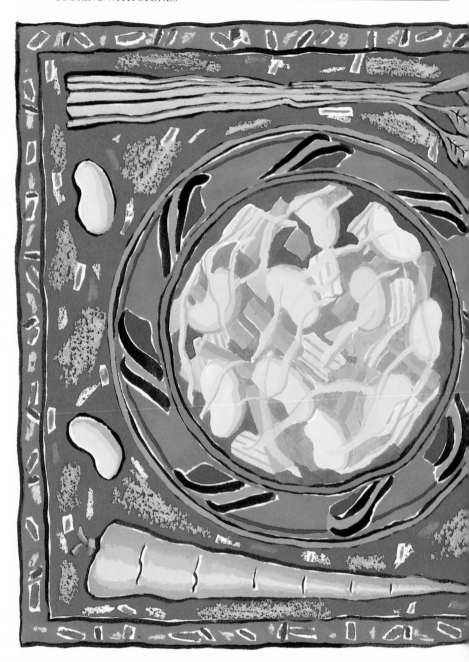

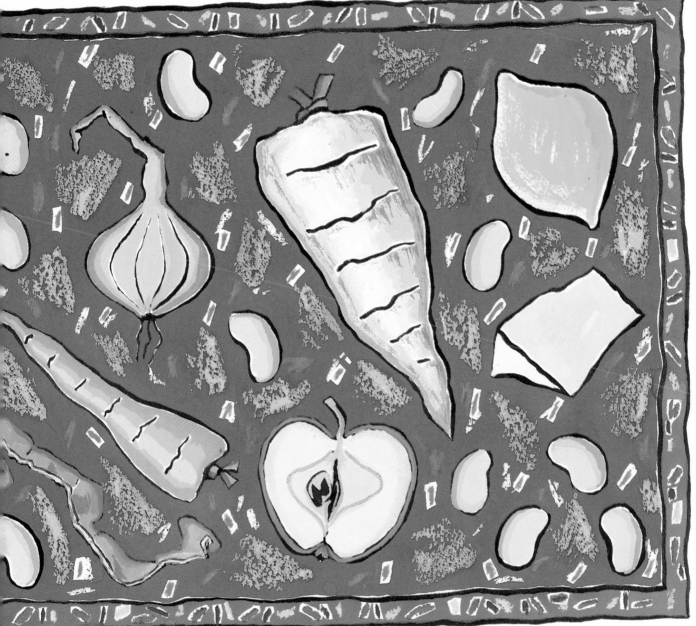

SALADS

Illustrations by Jessica Jenkins

Throughout English history, salad making has been regarded as a high art. Mystical powers have been attributed to a variety of leaves, fruits and herbs. John Evelyn, a notable grower and saladman, in his 'Acetaria' of 1699 recommends 'macerated dandelion leaf. 'Twas with this Hecate entertained Theseus'. Cucumber he favours '... to sharpen the appetite and cool the liver'. However, he states that garlic eating was considered fit punishment for crime!

A professional salad maker in the 1700s could expect to receive up to ten guineas for each salad prepared. In the nineteenth century, Disraeli's favourite was a salad of primrose shoots in a vinaigrette dressing (not to be recommended today unless you grow your own).

The 1920s and 1930s saw the salad rise to popular fashion in line with an interest in health and exercise, not unlike trends seen in the present decade. Many books published at that time reflect this and inspiration can still be found in attractive volumes concerned with gardening, cookery and healthy living. The modern salad maker can be seen foraging not only in greengrocer, garden and field, but also in antiquarian bookshops!

The 'Dig for Victory' campaign in Britain in the 1940s encouraged the growing of traditional saladings. The limited supplies obtainable on rations set people looking for wild foods both as a means of adding variety and also to supplement a basic yet adequate diet. How curious, then, to see a contemporary renewed interest in home grown and 'free' foods, when more hedgerow, meadow and downland have been destroyed since 1945 than at any time in our history.

Notwithstanding this despoliation, many farmers and growers are turning towards a less intensive, ecologically sound system of food production. It is most satisfying to see, even from the prairie like landscape of the north Wiltshire downs, new growers coming to us at Stones with organic produce. Without the use of inorganic fertilisers and pesticides, the crops develop a full flavour, often 'sweeter', as they contain less water; the shapes and colours of fruits, leaves and roots are more varied, as in the natural world. All things that matter very much indeed to the salad maker.

Success in the making of your own salads depends on your being aware not only of the seasons, but also of the temperature and weather conditions and even the time of day. Your personal tastes and moods cannot be excluded. These are all factors affecting the character of a salad and its appropriateness. As we are concerned with such a subtle and creative process, it seems unnecessary, in all but a few instances, to be dogmatic about measurements (lettuces refuse to be quantified) and which dressings to use. Instead, we offer a series of combinations that have worked well at Stones, but which are by no means finite. Sharpen a knife, hone your imagination, and begin.

DRESSINGS

Except for the mayonnaises and the avocado dressing, which require a food processor, and the heated marinade, the only piece of equipment you need here is a glass jar with a screw top lid (all the dressing recipes will fit comfortably into a 7 oz/200 gm instant coffee jar). Simply measure out the ingredients, and shake up in the jar. Store in or out of the fridge, and give the jar another good shake immediately before pouring.

LIGHT DRESSING

12 fl oz (350 ml) sunflower oil
4 fl oz (125 ml) lemon juice
4 fl oz (125 ml) white wine vinegar
1 teaspoon salt
1 teaspoon pepper
1 teaspoon mustard powder
1 teaspoon ground ginger
2 garlic cloves, crushed

DARK DRESSING

15 fl oz (425 ml) olive oil
5 fl oz (150 ml) red wine vinegar
1/2 teaspoon salt
1 teaspoon ground cumin
1 teaspoon ground coriander
1 large clove garlic, crushed

CHINESE DRESSING

12 fl oz (350 ml) pineapple juice
4 fl oz (125 ml) sunflower oil
3 tablespoons tamari
2 tablespoons sherry
1 teaspoon ground ginger
1 teaspoon Chinese 5 spice
1 tablespoon clear honey

AVOCADO DRESSING

1 avocado
1/4 pint (150 ml) soured cream or cottage cheese
good splash lemon juice
salt and pepper

Puree all ingredients together. Store in fridge.

HONEY & LEMON DRESSING

10 fl oz (300 ml) sunflower oil
7 fl oz (200 ml) lemon juice
2 tablespoons clear honey
pinch salt
pinch mustard powder
heaped teaspoon celery seed

MARINADE A LA GRECQUE

You can either pour this (still hot) over raw vegetables, or cook vegetables (very briefly) in the marinade.

8 fl oz (250 ml) water
4 fl oz (125 ml) white wine
4 fl oz (125 ml) olive oil
2 tablespoons lemon juice
1 teaspoon peppercorns
1 teaspoon coriander
1 clove garlic, crushed
2 teaspoons mixed herbs
1 bay leaf

Put all ingredients in a pan, and bring to boil. Simmer for 5 minutes.

CHINESE DRESSING WITH TAHINI

Good with rice salads or Chinese vegetables.

12 fl oz (350 ml) orange juice
4 fl oz (125 ml) sunflower oil
1 teaspoon tahini
3 tablespoons tamari
2 tablespoons sherry
2 teaspoons lemon juice
2 cloves garlic, crushed
1 teaspoon ground ginger

CITRUS VINAIGRETTE

10 fl oz (300 ml) olive oil
5 fl oz (150 ml) orange juice
5 fl oz (150 ml) lime juice
2 teaspoons crushed rosemary
salt and pepper

FRUITY VINAIGRETTE

This dressing is good with grains and fruit mixes.

8 fl oz (250 ml) olive oil
4 fl oz (125 ml) cider vinegar
4 fl oz (125 ml) apple (or other fruit)
concentrate
pinch of coriander
pinch of cumin
pinch of salt and pepper
pinch of poppy seeds

MAYONNAISE

Basic mayonnaise is so simple to make, and so satisfying, that one sometimes wonders at the high sales of commercial products. You can vary this recipe by adding a garlic clove or fresh herbs before the oil, using different mustards or substituting 2 tablespoons of tamari for 2 of the 3 spoons of vinegar. Add sauteed rhogan josh with the salt and pepper for a curry mayonnaise.

> *3 tablespoons white wine or cider vinegar*
> *2 teaspoons demerara sugar*
> *2 teaspoons coarse grained English mustard*
> *1 teaspoon salt*
> *½ teaspoon pepper*
> *1 egg*
> *1 pint (½ l) sunflower oil*

Blend all ingredients (except the oil) in a processor.

With the machine still running, slowly pour in the oil until it is all used up. Store in fridge.

LEMON-HERB-GARLIC MAYONNAISE

The herbs in this wonderful recipe can vary according to what is available in your garden, or from your greengrocer. If you can obtain them, hyssop and golden marjoram are particularly special. Do not attempt it with dried herbs!

> *4 tablespoons freshly squeezed lemon juice*
> *1 teaspoon salt*
> *½ teaspoon pepper*
> *1 teaspoon demerara sugar*
> *1 teaspoon mustard powder*
> *3 cloves garlic, peeled*
> *handful of fresh herbs*
> *2 eggs*
> *1 pint (½ l) sunflower oil*

Put all ingredients (except the oil) in order into a blender or processor bowl. Blend until the herbs and garlic are thoroughly incorporated.

While the blender is still running, slowly pour in the oil. Stop the machine as soon as all the oil has been added. Keep the resultant superlative mayonnaise refrigerated for up to 4 days (if you can resist it that long).

ROOT SALADS

Roots need only a good scrub and they can then be grated, on a medium to fine grater, by hand or processor. To preserve their flavour and nutrients they are best dressed immediately, whether you intend to eat the salad that day or leave it to marinate, covered and chilled, overnight.

Parsnips, turnips and swedes can all benefit from a light steaming or by being baked, scrubbed and whole, until soft, and then combined with raw vegetables, toasted nuts and seeds or cheeses for a heartier dish.

Grated celeriac and grated carrot.
Lemon juice, soured cream and horseradish sauce.

Grated parsnip, pine nuts and yellow peppers.
«Fruity vinaigrette».

Grated swede, walnuts and sauteed leek strips.
«Light dressing».

Grated kohlrabi, grated carrot and pumpkin seeds.
«Marinade a la Grecque».

Cubes of cooked parsnip, with chickpeas and chunks of well flavoured cheese.
«Dark dressing».

PASTA SALADS

Wholewheat pasta has a more interesting texture and far superior flavour than its paler counterpart. It is important to cook it 'al dente', drain immediately and briefly run cold water through it, before combining with your chosen dressing, herbs and other additions. The colour, flavour and texture of unrefined pasta make it the obvious choice for interesting salads.

Pasta shells, avocado cubes and radish slices.
Soured cream.

Pasta shells, grated Parmesan, French beans, red pepper strips, chopped fresh parsley and stuffed olives.
«Dark dressing».

Green tagliatelli, walnuts and thin slices of new carrots.
Walnut oil and sea salt.

Macaroni, black olives, marjoram, chopped fresh parsley, and diced red, green and yellow peppers.
«Citrus vinaigrette».

Macaroni, sliced mushrooms, oregano and sliced stuffed olives.
«Dark dressing».

Pasta shells, orange and yellow pepper strips, chopped fresh parsley and segments of orange.
«Light dressing».

Macaroni, sliced runner beans (lightly steamed, and steeped in the dressing to cool), poppy seeds and sliced red peppers.
«Marinade a la Grecque».

MAINLY GREEN SALADS

Wash and dry leaves carefully. Tear the softer lettuces by hand. The crisper varieties and leaves such as chard can be thinly sliced with a sharp blade. Dress when eating is imminent.

A glance through any wild foods manual will reveal many additions to the basic lettuce, watercress and endive formula. We have used new spring leaves from the lime trees around the restaurant *(Tilia europea)*, comfrey and young borage leaves, and a variety of cultivated and wild herbs. The combinations are limitless.

Red oak leaf lettuce, Chinese leaves, butterhead lettuce and salade frisee torn into pieces.
Tossed with a pinch of sea salt, one part lemon or lime juice and two parts walnut oil.

Spinach leaves torn into mouth sized pieces, avocado slices sprinkled with lemon juice and cubes of smoked tofu.
«Light dressing».

Young nasturtium leaves shredded with leaves of Swiss chard, with feta cheese crumbled over and nasturtium flowers to decorate.
Sea salt, olive oil and a squeeze of lemon juice.

Spinach and sorrel leaves, spring onions, crumbled Blue Cheshire or Stilton cheese.
«Light dressing».

Watercress, shredded iceberg lettuce and Chinese leaves.
Walnut oil and lime juice.

Swiss chard leaves, spinach, feta cheese and pine nuts.
Sesame oil and lemon juice.

Swiss chard, hard boiled eggs and smoked tofu.
«Light dressing».

Curly endive, red oak lettuce, Webbs lettuce, nasturtium leaves and borage flowers.
«Honey and lemon dressing».

Cauliflower and toasted cashew nuts.
Grain mustard and «mayonnaise».

Radiccio, Chinese leaves, Belgian chicory, sprouted mung beans and sprouted green lentils.
«Fruity vinaigrette».

Swiss chard leaves, Belgian endive, Chinese leaves, slices of fresh mango and smoked tofu.
Sunflower oil and a squeeze of lemon juice.

FRUIT BASED SALADS

It is helpful with these lighter salads to have an idea of the desired finished effect before you begin. Both shape and colour are key points here. Imagine, for example, thin slices from quartered dessert apples with their pink and yellow skins, or chunks of fruits and vegetables in primary colours. A handful of fresh herbs, toasted seeds or alfalfa sprouts can make a salad sparkle. Inspiration can be gleaned from paintings (not necessarily of food), phography, textiles, gardens and allotments, market stalls. In fact, any artful or accidental grouping of form and hue can fire the imagination. Attention to detail and the appropriate serving dish matter as much as the unadulterated freshness of your ingredients.

Tomatoes (quartered then halved), broad beans (lightly steamed and slipped from their grey skins) and fresh dill.
«Light dressing».

Sliced red skinned apples, thinly sliced pineapple, shredded red and white cabbage and fresh mint.
«Fruity vinaigrette».

Sliced green apples, sliced new carrots, baby sweet corn, strips of yellow pepper and sesame seeds.
«Chinese dressing».

Chopped fresh peaches, banana and celery slices, coconut and pumpkin seeds.
Soured cream and «mayonnaise».

Halved green grapes, orange slices, thinly sliced fennel and green pepper strips.
«Honey and lemon dressing».

Apple cubes, celery slices and brazil nuts.
Lemon juice and «mayonnaise».

Grated carrot, grated courgette and toasted sunflower seeds.
Orange juice and walnut oil.

Chunks of green apple, red cherries and sprouted mung beans.
«Citrus vinaigrette».

Grated carrot, coconut and currants (soaked in sherry).
Sesame oil.

Watermelon cubes, toasted sunflower seeds and shredded red cabbage.
«Citrus vinaigrette».

Tomatoes cut in chunks, sliced stuffed olives, cubes of feta cheese and blanched French beans.
«Dark dressing».

Mushroom slices, cucumber sticks, carrot sticks and fresh dill.
Natural yogurt.

Whole cherry tomatoes, steamed green beans and cubes of smoked tofu.
«Light dressing».

Carrots, celery, onion, tomato and cucumber, all diced small, with toasted sesame and sunflower seeds.
Cottage cheese and lemon juice.

Segments of pink grapefruit, shredded red cabbage, sliced spring onions, and sesame seeds, with red leaved lettuce lining the dish.
«Fruity vinaigrette».

Orange and avocado slices with toasted flaked almonds.
«Light dressing».

Tomato chunks, cubed cucumber, cubes of smoked tofu and fresh or dried tarragon.
«Light dressing».

Marrow slices (lightly cooked with white wine, dill seed and paprika), quartered tomatoes and sliced dill pickles.
Olive oil and sea salt.

Avocado cubes, sliced fennel and chopped hard boiled eggs.
Cider dressing.

Melon balls, pineapple in thin slices, shredded red and white cabbage and toasted sunflower and pumpkin seeds.
«Fruity vinaigrette».

Halved cucumber slices, cauliflower florets, diced red pepper and crumbled feta cheese.
«Light dressing».

Grated apple, grated courgette, plumped currants and toasted hazelnuts.
«Honey and lemon dressing».

Broccoli florets, sliced mushrooms, shredded red cabbage and pine nuts.
«Dark dressing».

Wax, runner and French beans, all steamed, and pine nuts.
«Light dressing».

Sliced golden courgettes, halved new carrots, lentil sprouts and sesame seeds.
«Honey and lemon dressing».

Cherry tomatoes, chopped broccoli florets and purple basil.
«Dark dressing».

59

GRAIN SALADS

Grains need to be well cooked, but not over done. Bulgar wheat, which is part cooked in its dry state, needs only boiling water poured over to moisten and after 15 minutes can be combined with other ingredients. Millet needs to be carefully cooked, as the moment between doneness and porridge is brief.

Brown basmati rice, diced onion and aubergine sautéed with mild curry spices, sliced spring onion, lime slices and toasted flaked almonds.
«Dark dressing».

Long grain brown rice, chickpeas, nectarine slices, halved grapes and mango chutney.
«Light dressing».

Wild rice, brown rice, baby corn strips, sliced marron mushrooms, crushed juniper berries, and onion sautéed with ground cardamom and ground cumin.
«Dark dressing».

Brown basmati rice, sultanas, arame, red pepper cubes, chopped parsley, flaked almonds, and onion sautéed with turmeric and Chinese 5 spice.
«Chinese dressing with tahini».

Rice, rye grains, mung beans, onion sautéed with paprika, dill, ground cumin, toasted hazelnuts and chopped parsley.
«Dark dressing».

Tabouleh: soaked bulgar wheat, chopped parsley, pine nuts.
Tamari, lemon juice and sunflower oil.

Cooked millet, grated carrot, diced red and green peppers and toasted sunflower seeds.
«Light dressing».

Rice, tamari, black olives, toasted hazelnuts and plumped sultanas.
«Fruity vinaigrette».

Millet, sautéed leeks, sliced red peppers.
«Honey and lemon dressing».

Rice, mango chutney, green grapes and toasted peanuts.
«Light dressing».

Rice and rye grains, walnuts, arame and plumped currants.
«Fruity vinaigrette».

Bulgar wheat, chopped fresh mint, crushed garlic and toasted peanuts.
Lemon juice and sunflower oil.

BEAN & LENTIL SALADS

The variety of colour to be found in the pulses is a most satisfying feature. Select ingredients to contrast or echo the shade of your chosen bean, pea or lentil. A glossy vinaigrette dressing adds to the jewel like effect.

Flageolet, haricot and red kidney beans, cauliflower florets and thin slices of green courgette.
«Dark dressing».

Flageolets, mung bean sprouts, broccoli florets and sliced button mushrooms.
«Light dressing».

Brown lentils, lexia raisins, sliced courgettes (yellow or green), onion and garlic sauteed in oil with ground coriander, cumin and cardamom.
«Dark dressing».

Aduki beans, turtle beans, red kidney beans, grated carrot, sliced spring onion and baby sweet corn.
«Chinese salad dressing».

Marinated chickpea sprouts, carrot, arame, and courgette and celery sticks.
«Chinese dressing with tahini».

Black kidney beans, flageolets, mangetout peas, strips of yellow pepper and baby sweet corn.
«Light dressing».

Buckwheat, green lentils, dried apricots and chopped parsley.
«Fruity vinaigrette».

Haricot and aduki beans, onion (sauteed with dill and cumin seeds), sliced mushrooms and tomato paste.
«Dark dressing».

Black kidney beans, grated root ginger, toasted sunflower seeds and cauliflower.
«Honey and lemon dressing».

Chickpeas, turtle beans, celery, and onion and aubergine sauteed with marjoram.
«Light dressing».

POTATO SALADS

The flavour of fresh organic potatoes needs little to enhance it: a pinch of sea salt, fresh milled pepper and some home made mayonnaise is hard to beat. The waxy red or slightly floury white potatoes are equally good, but take care not to over cook them.

Cornish new potatoes, diced onion sauteed with rhogan josh, cumin and coriander. Mango chutney and «mayonnaise».

Warm potatoes, cubed and dressed with olive oil and red wine vinegar, crushed garlic and sea salt.
Fresh tarragon and «mayonnaise» folded in when cool.

Warm potatoes quartered in red wine and walnut oil and meaux mustard, marinated overnight. Capers and chopped parsley added when ready to serve.

New potatoes and chopped mixed herbs (eg chives, marjoram, lovage).
«Mayonnaise» and a dash of «light dressing».

Sliced warm potatoes, thinly sliced celery and sauteed cumin, garlic and poppy seeds. Natural yogurt.

Sliced potatoes, sliced celery, sliced dill pickles, fresh coriander and snipped chives.
Soured cream, natural yogurt and coarse grained mustard.

Potato cubes and dill pickles (or capers). Apple and thyme jelly and «mayonnaise».

PORTABLE SAVOURIES

Illustrations by Caroline della Porta

Picnic, car or train journey, fell walking or not sure you'll find a reasonable eating place when visiting a town? Best be prepared with these recipes which travel well, and are easily packed into bags or boxes. Together with fresh fruit, perhaps a small tub of salad and a biscuit or cake, you need only a flask of your favourite beverage and you can go anywhere!

FRENCH BEAN & PECAN PATE

Excellent as a dip for hot «sesame pitta bread», or for raw vegetables. You need a food processor for this one.

1 onion, finely chopped
1 tablespoon sunflower oil
8 oz (225 gm) French beans, topped and steamed until tender
2 eggs, hard boiled
4 oz (100 gm) toasted pecans
4 tablespoons dry white wine
2 tablespoons mayonnaise
juice of 1 lime

Saute the onion gently in oil until transparent. Put all the ingredients in the bowl of a food processor, and blend until smooth. Check seasonings. Turn into another container, and refrigerate, covered, for at least 2 hours.

SPICY LENTIL & CHEDDAR CROQUETTES

Makes 9.

8 oz (225 gm) red lentils
a few bay leaves
1 pint (550 ml) water

1 teaspoon garam masala
½ teaspoon chilli powder
2 teaspoons ground coriander
1 teaspoon ground cumin
2 oz (50 gm) margarine
1 very large onion, finely chopped
3 large cloves garlic, crushed
2 large carrots, finely chopped
2 green peppers, finely chopped

3 tablespoons tomato paste
12 oz (350 gm) cheddar, grated
2 eggs, beaten

Simmer the lentils gently with the bay leaves until all the water is absorbed. Cool, and remove the leaves.

Saute the spices in the margarine on medium heat for 2 minutes. Add all the vegetables and stir fry for 5 minutes.

Take off heat and turn into a large bowl. Add the lentils and the tomato paste. Mix everything well together and season to taste. Stir in the cheese and the eggs. Leave to go completely cold, then form into 9 round, ¾ inch (2 cm) thick cakes.

Line a baking sheet with baking parchment and put the croquettes on top. Bake at 160° for 20-25 minutes, until firm. Serve with cucumber raita, crisp green salad and steamed rice.

SESAME PITTA BREAD

These are delicious hot or cold. Makes 6 large pittas for 6 hungry people.

9 fl oz (250 ml) hot water
1 tablespoon dried yeast
1 tablespoon clear honey
2 oz (50 gm) strong white flour
2 tablespoons olive oil
½ teaspooon salt
4 oz (100 gm) wholewheat flour
4 oz (100 gm) toasted sesame seeds
about 7 oz (200 gm) additional wholewheat flour
2 tablespoons olive oil for oiling bowl

Put water, yeast and honey in a large bowl and leave to stand for about 5 minutes, until frothy.

Stir in the next 5 ingredients and beat 100 times (or 3 minutes with a dough hook in a mixer).

Now, work in enough additional flour to make a pliable, but not sticky dough. Turn onto a well floured board and knead until smooth and bouncy. Put oil into a clean bowl, and transfer the dough. Turn it over and over to completely coat with the oil. Leave to rise in a warm place until double in bulk (about 1 hour).

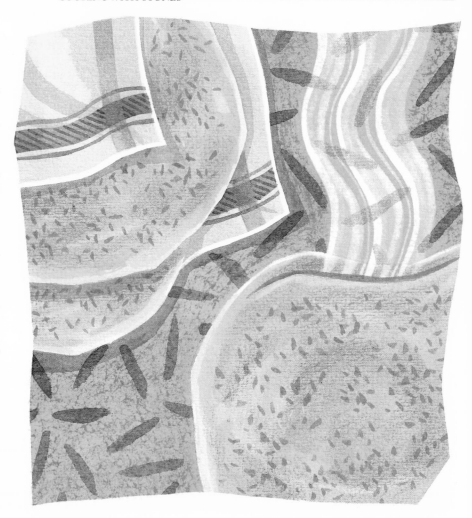

Divide into 6 equal sized pieces, and roll each on a well floured board with an equally well floured rolling pin, until circles of about 8 inch (20 cm) diameter, each about ¼ inch (5 mm) thick are achieved. Place 2 pittas on each of 3 well oiled or papered baking sheets, and leave to rest for 5 minutes, while your oven is heating to 190°. Now, pop all the circles into the oven at once and bake for 3 minutes. Open the oven, turn the pittas over and bake 3 minutes on the other side. Take out of the oven, and slit open along a short side while they are still puffed up. Then wrap in a clean tea towel, to prevent them from drying out.

GOOD THINGS FOR FILLING PITTA POCKETS

Pitta breads are pockets just waiting for your imagination to jump in. Here are a few ideas to help you along.

You can also refer to the salad section. Any of the lighter salad combinations are perfectly complemented by pitta bread.

Left over «refried beans» mixed with left over tomato sauce, sauteed onion, raisins and toasted flaked almonds, seasoned with oregano, cumin, chilli powder, salt and pepper. Top with diced or grated cheese, shredded Chinese leaves, tomato slices and yogurt.

Avocado mashed with grated Red Leicester cheese, crushed garlic, cashew butter and yogurt. Top with toasted cashews and finely chopped onion.

Tasty apple (such as Cox) chunks, smoked tofu and sharp cheddar cubes stirred into mustardy mayonnaise. Top with finely shredded spinach.

Chopped hard boiled eggs, sliced celery and a little finely chopped onion, stirred with mayonnaise and chutney, topped with crisp lettuce.

Button mushrooms sauteed until tender in butter with a crushed garlic clove, a little finely chopped onion, a pinch of thyme and a dash each of tamari and lemon juice. Top with hard boiled egg slices and a little finely chopped smoked tofu.

Crunchy peanut butter blended with mango chutney. Top with fresh pineapple and banana slices and lots of alfalfa sprouts.

Fromage frais blended with a little Blue Stilton and the zest and juice of an orange. Top with chopped dates and banana slices rolled in soured cream, then toasted coconut.

69

RED LENTIL & SINGLE GLOUCESTER SQUARES WITH FRESH THYME

Makes 9 squares.

8 oz (225 gm) red lentils
½ pint (300 ml) water
1 onion, very finely chopped
1 tablespoon chopped fresh thyme
1 large handful chopped fresh parsley
2 teaspoons ground cumin
pinch cayenne
7 oz (200 gm) Single Gloucester cheese, grated
3 eggs
4 fl oz (100 ml) tomato juice

Put lentils in water, bring to boil and simmer for about 7 minutes, until the water is mostly absorbed and the lentils are just tender. Take off the heat and allow to stand until all the water has gone.

Mix the onion, herbs, spices and cheese with the lentils. Beat the eggs with the tomato juice and stir into the lentil mix. Season to taste.

Turn into a shallow dish lined with baking parchment, and bake at 170° for about 35 minutes, until firm. Cut into squares when cold.

CHEESE & MUSHROOM PIES

Makes 6 individual pies.

1 quantity «basic pastry»
1 small onion, chopped
1 clove garlic, crushed
1 oz (25 gm) margarine
4 oz (100 gm) mushrooms, sliced thin
2 tablespoons lemon juice
4 oz (100 gm) wholewheat breadcrumbs
1 oz (25 gm) toasted sunflower seeds
1 oz (25 gm) toasted sesame seeds
1 large handful chopped fresh parsley
8 oz (225 gm) cottage cheese
8 oz (225 gm) cheddar, grated

Make the pastry, and line 6 pie pans 3½ inches/9 cm in diameter (use slightly less than half the pastry for this).

Gently saute the onion and garlic in the margarine, until the onion is transparent. Add the mushrooms and lemon juice and stir until the mushrooms are all coated with the margarine. Take off the heat.

Stir in the crumbs and the seeds, the parsley and the cheeses. Check the seasoning. Fill the lined pie pans equally with the mixture, and lid with the rest of the pastry. Brush with egg, and bake at 170° for 20-25 minutes until golden brown.

SAVOURY ROLLS

Delicious eaten hot or cold with your favourite chutney or savoury jelly. Depending on how long you make them, this recipe will give you anything from a dozen to 20 rolls.

8 oz (225 gm) chopped nuts
4 oz (125 gm) mashed potato
4 onions, chopped and sauteed
2 teaspoons yeast extract
1 tablespoon sage
1 tablespoon basil
salt and pepper

8 oz (225 gm) «basic pastry»
egg for brushing
sesame seeds

Combine the filling ingredients in a bowl. If you cut your onions in a processor, drain off the water before frying, or the mix will be too wet. Check seasonings.

Roll out the pastry into a rectangle 15 inches (40 cm) wide. Make a sausage of filling along the width, ½ inch (1 cm) from the edge. Roll the pastry over, with the filling, and seal the edge where the end strip contacts the main sheet, by brushing with egg. Cut along the seal line, to remove a long filled roll. Repeat the process, laying out a strip of filling, rolling over the pastry and sealing and cutting away, until you get to the end of the pastry sheet. Then cut the long sausages into individual rolls, and slash the tops. Brush them with egg, scatter over some sesame seeds and bake at 170° for 25-30 minutes, until golden brown.

71

FALAFEL

Makes 18-20 of these morish Middle Eastern chickpea croquettes.

1 lb (450 gm) cooked chickpeas
4 fl oz (100 ml) water
2 tablespoons soya flour
2 oz (50 gm) wholewheat breadcrumbs
2 handfuls chopped fresh parsley
2 teaspoons ground cumin
1 tablespoon turmeric
2 tablespoons dried basil
2 tablespoons dried marjoram
2 tablespoons light tahini
1 teaspoon cayenne pepper
1-2 teaspoons salt
2 teaspoons pepper
5 eggs, beaten
olive oil

Grind the chickpeas together with the water in your processor. Turn into a bowl and stir in all the other dry ingredients. Bind with the eggs, and check the seasoning. Form into golf sized balls and place on a well oiled baking sheet. Drizzle each one with a few drops of oil, and bake at 160° for about 20 minutes, until just firm.

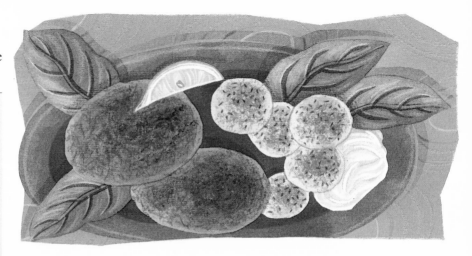

EGGHOGS

Little brown things in jackets are not infrequently seen in the restaurant, sniffing around the bowls of salads. A good, free ranging egg should always be well dressed, and with this recipe, can face up to the very best company. Makes 8.

2 tablespoons sunflower oil
1 onion, finely chopped
1 clove garlic, crushed
1 carrot, finely chopped
1 green pepper, finely chopped
8 oz (225 gm) red lentils

½ pint (300 ml) cold water
1 tablespoon vegetable stock concentrate
2 tablespoons tomato paste
4 oz (100 gm) mixed chopped nuts
4 oz (100 gm) wholemeal breadcrumbs
½ tablespoon each of basil, thyme and oregano
1 egg

8 eggs, hard boiled and peeled
olive oil for coating

Gently saute onion, garlic and carrot in oil for 5 minutes or until onion is tender. Add pepper, and continue to saute. A minute later, add lentils and cook for another minute, stirring all the time.

Pour in water, a little at a time, as mix absorbs liquid. Stir constantly. When lentils are soft (but definitely not mushy), remove from heat and stir in stock concentrate, tomato paste, nuts, breadcrumbs and herbs. Beat in the raw egg.

To coat the hard boiled eggs, take some of the mixture in your hand and mould it around the egg, encasing the egg in a jacket about ½ inch (1 cm) thick. Make sure there are no gaps or cracks.

Place eggs on a parchment lined baking sheet, dribble a little olive oil over the top and bake at 160° for 20 minutes. Eat cold with chutney of the best quality.

MUNG BEAN & PEPPER CROQUETTES WITH CORIANDER

Makes 12 croquettes.

1 onion, finely chopped
2 large cloves garlic, crushed
2 tablespoons sunflower oil
1 small red and 1 small green pepper, finely chopped

8 oz (225 gm) mung beans, soaked and boiled until soft
1 handful chopped fresh parsley
a few sprigs fresh coriander, finely chopped
1 scant teaspoon chilli powder
2 tablespoons tomato paste
½ teaspoon salt
1 egg, beaten

oil for drizzling

Saute the onion and garlic in oil, gently, until the onion is transparent. Add the peppers and stir fry until the latter are just crisp and tender. Turn into a large bowl.

Mash the mung beans and add them to the vegetable saute. Stir in the herbs, the chilli powder, the tomato paste and salt. Mix until everything is well acquainted. Bind with the beaten egg.

Form the mixture into 12 small croquettes, each about ½ inch (1 cm) thick. Arrange on a well oiled baking sheet and drizzle each one with a little extra oil. Bake at 170° for about 20 minutes or until just firm. Serve hot or cold with yogurt and cucumber.

HARVEST VEGETABLE QUICHE

You can vary the filling according to what you have in your garden or the choices from the market at the end of summer.

1 quantity «basic pastry»
3 tablespoons sunflower oil
1 large onion, chopped
1 clove garlic, crushed
1 bunch carrots, sliced
3 courgettes, sliced
4 oz (100 gm) mangetout peas
1 lb (450 gm) mushrooms, sliced
1 tablespoon tamari
12 oz (350 gm) cheddar, grated
7 eggs
1/4 pint (150 ml) milk
salt and pepper
3 tablespons single cream

Line greased flan dish with quiche pastry.

Heat oil in a saucepan. Saute all vegetables together, except mushrooms, until onion softens.

Fold in sliced mushrooms. Remove from heat and add tamari.

Cover pastry base with half the cheese, then vegetables, then remaining cheese. Beat together egg, milk, salt and pepper, and pour over. Gently pour cream into centre of quiche. Bake at 140° for 50 minutes, until golden and firm in the middle.

SMOKED TOFU & TEIFI QUICHE

A delicious aroma wafts from the oven as this cooks.

1 quantity «basic pastry»
2 oz (50 gm) sesame seeds
1 pack smoked tofu, cut into large chunks
2 oz (50 gm) fresh parsley, chopped
4 oz (100 gm) baby sweetcorn
12 oz (350 gm) Teifi cheese, grated
7 eggs
7 fl oz (200 ml) milk
salt and pepper

Make up a quantity of pastry with the sesame seeds, adding them in with the flour. Line a greased flan dish.

Arrange tofu and parsley on base. Place the sweetcorn in a star pattern on top, and sprinkle with cheese.

Beat together eggs, milk, salt and pepper and pour over the quiche. Bake at 150° for 45 minutes.

FRENCH BEAN PROVENCAL

For extra finesse, use walnut oil and stoned black olives with the cheese topping.

1 quantity «nut pastry» made with walnuts
2 tablespoons sunflower oil
2 red and 2 green peppers, sliced
2 garlic cloves, crushed
1 onion, sliced
1 teaspoon each basil, marjoram, thyme
10 oz (275 gm) cheese (Teifi or cheddar), grated
8 oz (225 gm) lightly cooked French beans
7 eggs
7 fl oz (200 ml) milk
salt and pepper

Line a greased dish with pastry.

Cook peppers, onion, garlic and herbs in oil until onion softens.

Sprinkle half cheese on pastry base, then pepper mix, beans, remaining cheese and egg mix (eggs, milk and seasonings). Bake at 150° for 45 minutes.

COURGETTE & TOMATO QUICHE WITH WALNUT CRUST

Nutty pastry has a delicious crumbly texture, an appropriate foil to the most savoury filling.

1 quantity «nut pastry» made with walnuts
3 tablespoons olive oil
1 large onion, chopped
2 cloves garlic, crushed
6 good sized courgettes, sliced
2 teaspoons oregano
8 oz (225 gm) Red Leicester cheese, grated
3 large tomatoes, sliced
6 eggs
pint (150 ml) milk
salt and pepper

Heat oil in a saucepan and saute onion, garlic and sliced courgettes until onion softens. Add oregano. Remove from heat.

In flan dish lined with walnut pastry, layer half the cheese, then courgette mix, slices of tomato and the rest of the cheese.

Beat together egg, milk and seasonings, and pour over the quiche. Cook at 160° for 45 minutes.

MUSHROOM QUICHE WITH SPINACH CRUST

A pretty speckled slice.

¾ lb (350 gm) fresh spinach
1 oz (25 gm) butter

8 oz (225 gm) strong white flour
8 oz (225 gm) porridge oats
2 eggs
pinch salt
nutmeg, grated

Begin by making the crust. Cook spinach in butter over a high heat until limp. Process in blender for 10 seconds, and place in bowl.

Add flour, oats, eggs, salt and nutmeg and mix with a fork. Press into oiled flan dish with floured fingers. Bake at 150° for 20 minutes, until firm. Meanwhile, make the filling.

---

1 oz (25 gm) margarine
1 onion, chopped
1½ lb (700 gm) mushrooms, sliced
1 tablespoon lemon juice
3 tablespoons wholewheat flour

2 eggs
1 cup natural yogurt
salt and pepper
1 oz (25 gm) fresh parsley, chopped
9 oz (250 gm) cheddar, grated

Melt margarine in saucepan, and saute onion until soft. Add mushroom and lemon juice. Cook for 5 minutes. Add flour and cook for 8 more minutes. Remove from heat.

Beat eggs with yogurt and seasoning. Add to mushrooms in saucepan with cheese and parsley. Mix well and pour into spinach crust. Cook at 150° for 40 minutes.

FRENCH BEAN & TOMATO QUICHE

The beans are briefly steamed to keep their 'bite' and bright colour. Runner beans or wax beans could be an alternative.

---

1 quantity «nut pastry» made with pecans
12 oz (350 gm) Teifi cheese, grated
6 tomatoes, sliced
12 oz (350 gm) lightly cooked French beans
7 eggs
7 fl oz (200 ml) milk
salt and pepper

Line greased dish with pastry.

Sprinkle half the cheese over pastry, top with half the tomato slices, then the beans, the rest of the tomato and the remaining cheese.

Pour over egg mix (eggs, milk and seasonings). Bake at 150° for 45 minutes.

CAULIFLOWER, ONION & NUTMEG QUICHE

Avoid ready grated nutmeg, but grate your own freshly for a lovely aromatic savour.

1 quantity «basic pastry»
1 medium onion, chopped
1 oz (25 gm) margarine
1 cauliflower (1½ lb/700 gm), divided into florets
¼ nutmeg, grated
½ pint (300 ml) milk
12 oz (350 gm) Devon Oke cheese, grated
8 eggs
salt and pepper

Line greased flan dish with pastry.

Saute onion in margarine until soft. Add cauliflower and nutmeg. Cook for 5 minutes. Add milk, cover and simmer for 10 minutes or until cauliflower is just tender. Drain, and reserve milk.

Sprinkle 5 oz (150 gm) cheese over the lined dish, then cauliflower, then rest of cheese. Beat together eggs, salt and pepper, and the cauliflower milk, and pour over quiche. Bake at 160° for 45 minutes.

BROCCOLI & RED PEPPER QUICHE

The reds and greens look bright and attractive.

1 quantity «basic pastry»
9 oz (250 gm) cooked broccoli florets
1 red pepper, sliced
12 oz (350 gm) Red Leicester cheese, grated
6 eggs
7 fl oz (200 ml) milk
salt and pepper

Line greased dish with pastry.

Sprinkle half cheese onto base, arrange broccoli and pepper slices on top. Cover with second half of cheese.

Mix together eggs, milk and seasonings, and pour over quiche. Bake at 150° for 45 minutes.

COURGETTE & FRESH DILL QUICHE

Dill is easy to grow in a sunny spot with attention to watering. A versatile herb and very delicate in appearance.

1 quantity «nut pastry» made with almonds
2 tablespoons sunflower oil
8 courgettes, thinly sliced
handful fresh dill, chopped (or ½ oz/15 gm dried)
12 oz (350 gm) Red Leicester cheese, grated
7 eggs
7 fl oz (200 ml) milk
salt and pepper

Line greased dish with pastry.

Saute courgettes in oil for 10 minutes. Add dill.

Sprinkle half cheese on base, then courgettes and remaining cheese. Beat together eggs, milk and seasoning and pour over. Bake at 150° for 45 minutes.

SPINACH QUICHE WITH POTATO-ONION CRUST

This quiche is best made in a cast iron or enamelled dish to obtain a crisp crust.

1½ lb (700 gm) potato, grated
1 teaspoon salt
2 eggs, beaten
3 tablespoons onion, grated

First make the crust. Place potato in colander and sprinkle with salt, which will draw out water. Leave to drain for 20 minutes. Squeeze out excess moisture, and combine potato with eggs and onion. Line a well greased flan dish with the mix, pressing it carefully into the base and sides.

1 onion, chopped
1 clove garlic, crushed
2 oz (50 gm) butter
1 lb (450 gm) fresh spinach
10 oz (275 gm) Red Leicester cheese, grated
¼ pint (150 ml) milk
7 eggs
salt and pepper
¼ nutmeg, grated

Saute onion and garlic in butter. When soft, add spinach and cook quickly. Remove from heat when the spinach leaves start to wilt.

Put 4 oz (100 gm) grated cheese on the quiche base, then onion and spinach. Beat together eggs, milk, salt, pepper and nutmeg, and pour over. Top with remaining cheese. Bake at 160° for 50 minutes, until golden and firm in the centre.

QUICHE PROVENCAL

This quiche is also good made with the red skinned variety of onion and sprigs of fresh herbs.

1 quantity «basic pastry»
3 tablespoons olive oil
1 large onion, sliced
2 fat cloves garlic, crushed
1 yellow, 2 red and 2 green peppers, sliced
1 teaspoon each marjoram, thyme and basil
8 eggs
¼ pint (150 ml) milk
salt and pepper
12 oz (350 gm) Devon Oke cheese, grated

Line greased dish with pastry.

Heat oil in saucepan and saute onion, garlic, peppers and herbs until softening.

Beat together egg, milk, salt and pepper.

Put half of the cheese on the pastry base, then pepper mix, rest of cheese and finally the egg and milk. Bake at 150° for 40 minutes, or until golden and firm in the centre.

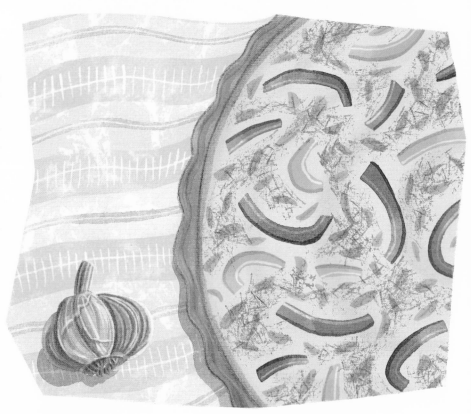

BROCCOLI & STILTON QUICHE

Delicious too made with Blue Cheshire or the rare Blue Vinney cheese.

1 quantity «nut pastry» made with walnuts
1½ lb (700 gm) cooked broccoli
12 oz (350 gm) blue Stilton cheese, crumbled
7 eggs
7 fl oz (200 ml) milk
salt and pepper

Line greased dish with pastry.

Sprinkle half cheese over pastry, arrange broccoli on top, then add remaining cheese.

Mix together eggs, milk and seasonings, and pour over quiche. Bake at 150° for 45 minutes.

CAULIFLOWER & MUSHROOM QUICHE

Wholewheat crumbs mean a more substantially filling quiche. Ideal served warm for a winter evening supper with a hearty soup and crisp salad!

1 quantity «basic pastry»
1 lb (450 gm) cauliflower florets
1 onion, sliced
1 garlic clove, finely crushed
2 tablespoons sunflower oil
1½ lb (700 gm) mushrooms
5 oz (150 gm) wholewheat breadcrumbs
1 teaspoon basil
5 fl oz (150 ml) milk
8 eggs
salt and pepper
12 oz (350 gm) cheddar, grated

Line greased dish with pastry.

Steam cauliflower until tender, and put aside.

Saute onion and garlic in oil until onion is soft. Add mushrooms and saute briefly. Stir in crumbs and basil.

Beat together eggs, milk, salt and pepper, and add to mushroom mix.

Layer cauliflower in the dish on top of half of the cheese. Pour over mushroom mix, and top with remainder of cheddar. Bake at 160° for 45 minutes.

SAUCES

Illustrations by Felicity Roma Bowers

Most of the sauces and marinades in this section are called for in the megalith chapter, but their use need not be so restricted! Try «fresh basil sauce» (a lighter version of «pesto») over steamed or sauteed summer vegetables and cooked pasta; «redcurrant-orange», and «spiced apricot» sauces go well with roasts, but try them also with sauteed pressed tofu, croquettes or other light savouries; «rich mushroom-sherry sauce», again good with roasts, also complements the flavour of lightly steamed vegetables such as artichokes or celeriac; try using any of the tomato or peanut based sauces over cooked beans or pasta, or to fill jacket potatoes, and top with cheese. «Ratatouille» is perfect with hard boiled or poached eggs. Use the various marinades for vegetables instead of tofu, to create unusual salads. Look out for more suggestions at the beginnings of the recipes, and invent combinations of sauces and ingredients of your own!

LIGHT WHITE WINE–TOMATO SAUCE

You can vary this recipe by substituting milk or cream for some of the wine, or completely replacing the wine with milk and stock, and spiking up with a splash of cognac.

1 large onion, chopped
4 sticks celery, finely sliced
4 cloves garlic, crushed
a few bay leaves
4 tablespoons olive oil
2 small red and 2 small green peppers, finely chopped
about 4-5 oz (125 gm) wholewheat flour
10 tomatoes, pureed
1 tablespoon dried marjoram
2 teaspoons dried basil
9 fl oz (250 ml) white wine

Saute the onion, celery and garlic with the bay leaves in the oil, until the onion is transparent. Stir in the peppers and continue to saute 2 minutes longer. Stir in just enough flour to absorb the juices in the pan, and cook 1 minute longer. Add the tomatoes and the dried herbs and the wine and simmer until thick. Season to taste.

MUSHROOM–WHITE WINE SAUCE

A light sauce to accompany roasts or serve over filled pancakes.

1 small onion, finely chopped
1 oz (25 gm) margarine
12 oz (350 gm) mushrooms, ¾ chopped, ¼ left whole
2 teaspoons dried thyme
1½ tablespoons arrowroot
½ pint (300 ml) vegetable stock
¼ pint medium dry white wine
tamari, pepper and lemon juice to season

Saute the onion in the margarine for 2 minutes. Add the mushrooms and thyme, and cook, stirring, for a further minute. Cream the arrowroot with a little of the stock, then add the rest of the stock and the wine to the mushrooms. Simmer 10 minutes, then add the arrowroot cream and stir until the sauce has thickened. Season to taste.

REDCURRANT–ORANGE SAUCE

10 oz (275 gm) fresh or frozen redcurrants
zest and juice of 2 oranges
3 oz (75 gm) demerara sugar
1 teaspoon arrowroot
1 tablespoon cardamom
pinch allspice

Simmer the redcurrants with the orange zest, the juice of 1 orange and the sugar for 5 minutes, stirring until the sugar has dissolved. Meanwhile, blend the arrowroot with the juice of the second orange and spices. Stir the arrowroot mixture into the redcurrants and simmer until thick and glossy. Take off heat and serve warm or chilled.

FRESH BASIL SAUCE

3 spring onions, chopped
large handful of fresh basil leaves
small handful chopped fresh parsley
1 tablespoon olive oil
2 tablespoons grated Parmesan cheese
(optional)
6 large tomatoes
1 tablespoon lemon juice
1 teaspoon tamari
tomato juice (optional)

Whirl all the ingredients, except the tomato juice and seasonings, in a food processor. Thin as required with the juice and season to taste. Serve warm or cold.

PESTO

Stir into hot, lightly buttered pasta for a classically simple, delicious summer supper. The final touch in «soupe au pistou».

small handful fresh basil (green or purple)
2 fat cloves garlic
2 tablespoons grated Parmesan cheese
small handful pine nuts
1 tablespoon olive oil
pinch pepper and salt

Whizz all ingredients in blender. Store in fridge tightly sealed.

MORE THAN BASIC TOMATO SAUCE

This is a sauce with many uses. Layer it with lasagne verdi and spinach, and top with a thick cheese sauce; mix with cooked beans or lentils and use as a layer in a «Rainbow pie»; stir into cooked noodles and top with grated cheese for a quick pasta supper; use as an alternative to «pizza sauce»; etc. The flavour can be altered by adding different spices or by using different herbs. Try lots and lots of fresh basil for a truly luxurious sauce. The recipe makes 2 pints (1100 ml), and the sauce freezes well.

2 large onions, chopped
5 sticks celery, chopped
3 carrots, chopped
3 large cloves garlic, crushed
1 tablespoon sunflower oil
1 tablespoon olive oil
1 oz (25 gm) light muscovado sugar
1 tablespoon dried basil
1 tablespoon dried marjoram
7 fl oz (200 ml) cider vinegar
6 large tomatoes, chopped
8 fl oz (250 ml) tomato paste
7 fl oz (200 ml) vegetable stock

Saute all vegetables, except tomatoes, in oils until onion and carrot are softening. Keep the pan covered, on low heat.

Add sugar, herbs and vinegar amd simmer uncovered for about 30 minutes, until vegetables are cooked and sauce is reduced. Season to taste with tamari and pepper.

Add tomatoes, paste and stock, and simmer for another 30 minutes. Remove from heat, and check seasonings.

THICK CHEESE SAUCE

You can of course thin this by adding more milk.

1 pint (550 ml) milk
a few bay leaves
large pinch of ground cloves
1½ oz (40 gm) margarine
1½ oz (40 gm) wholewheat flour
½ teaspoon mustard powder
pinch of cayenne
dash of tamari
12 oz (350 gm) farm cheese of your choice, grated
salt and pepper to taste

Warm the milk with the bay leaves and cloves.

Melt the margarine on gentle heat and stir in the flour. Cook for 1 minute, stirring. Gradually add the warm milk (after removing the bay leaves), stirring all the time, and simmer, still stirring, until a thick, smooth sauce is achieved.

Stir in the mustard powder, cayenne and tamari, then the cheese. Season to taste.

BRIE & RED PEPPER SAUCE

1 large red pepper, cut into short strips
splash of sunflower oil for saute
8 oz (225 gm) Sharpham Brie cheese
2 tablespoons soured cream
1 teaspoon lemon juice
4 tablespoons milk

Saute the pepper strips very gently, until just beginning to soften. Remove from heat. Puree the Brie with the soured cream, lemon juice and milk. Stir in the pepper strips and store in the fridge until required. Serve at room temperature.

LENTIL–CIDER SAUCE

This is a wonderful sauce for lasagne. Try layering it with mushrooms cooked in cider, sauteed courgettes and a rich cheese sauce. The recipe will make enough for 2 lasagnes. The sauce freezes well.

9 oz (250 gm) brown lentils
1 pint (500 ml) cider
a few bay leaves

1 very large onion, finely chopped
3 cloves garlic, crushed
3 carrots, grated
3 sticks celery, finely chopped
2 tablespoons olive oil

12 fl oz (350 ml) cider
8 fl oz (200 ml) water
2 teaspoons vegetable stock concentrate

1 green and 1 red pepper, chopped into little squares
1 cooking apple, grated
4½ oz (125 gm) mushrooms, roughly chopped
2 tablespoons tomato paste

Simmer the lentils very slowly, covered, with the bay leaves in the cider for about 45 minutes, or until the lentils are tender but still have a 'bite'. Check the pan occasionally, and add a little water if the lentils show any signs of sticking. Take off the heat and set aside with any residual liquid.

In another pan, gently saute the hard vegetables in a little olive oil for 15 minutes.

Make up the stock with the cider, water and concentrate and add with the rest of the ingredients (except the reserved lentils!) and simmer, covered, until everything is tender. Remove from the heat and add the lentils. Season to taste.

RICH MUSHROOM–SHERRY SAUCE

12 oz (350 gm) mushrooms
2 sticks celery, sliced small
2 carrots, chopped small
2 cloves garlic, crushed
2 oz (50 gm) margarine
wholewheat flour
1 pint (600 ml) vegetable stock
a few bay leaves
4 tablespoons sherry
tamari and pepper

RATATOUILLE

We always serve ratatouille as an accompanying sauce rather than as a dish in its own right. Try it with mushrooms and almonds as a pancake filling, or as the base for a quick mousssaka. Makes about 2½ pints (1½ l).

1 beautiful, large firm aubergine
olive oil for brushing tray
2 large onions, coarsely chopped
6 cloves garlic, crushed
4 tablespoons olive oil
12 bay leaves
3 courgettes, sliced
6 tomatoes, sliced
2 green and 1 red pepper, sliced into thin strips
12 fl oz (350 ml) good quality dry white wine
4 tablespoons tomato paste
2 tablespoons dried basil
1 tablespoon dried marjoram
½ teaspoon pepper
1 teaspoon salt

Split the aubergine lengthways, and put both halves, cut surface down, onto a well oiled baking sheet. Bake in a hot (200°) oven for about 10 minutes, or until the flesh is just choppable. Chop into 1 inch (2 cm) cubes, and set aside.

Stir the onions and garlic in the olive oil on medium heat for 5 minutes, or until the onion is transparent and softening. Add the bay leaves, courgettes, tomatoes, peppers and reserved aubergine cubes, and cook gently (turn heat down) for 10 minutes, covered.

Add the wine and tomato paste, and continue to simmer on very low heat, covered, for about 30 minutes, until everything is just tender. Remove from heat, and stir in the dried herbs and seasonings. Cool and refrigerate for at least 12 hours before using.

Gently saute vegetables and garlic, covered, in margarine until tender. Uncover, and gradually sprinkle in flour until all liquid is absorbed. Cook a further minute, stirring. Gradually add stock, stirring continuously. Add bay leaves and simmer until thick. Remove from heat.

At this point, the sauce can be cooled and refrigerated, or potted and frozen.

To complete (after reheating if necessary), add sherry and adjust seasoning with tamari and pepper.

CIDER SAUCE

This is a sharp sauce for covering stir fried or steamed vegetables, to be served with plain boiled brown rice or boulangere potatoes. If you find it too sharp, stir in some redcurrant jelly to taste.

1 large onion, chopped
2 carrots, finely chopped
2 large cloves garlic, crushed
1 tablespoon dill seed
2 tablespoons sunflower oil
2 tablespoons wholewheat flour
½ pint (300 ml) dry cider
2 tablespoons tamari
1-2 teaspoons redcurrant jelly (optional)

Saute the onion, carrots and garlic gently with the dill until the onion is transparent and the carrots beginning to be tender. Add the flour and cook 30 seconds. Gradually stir in the cider and cook gently until a glossy sauce is achieved. Season to taste.

PIZZA SAUCE

Do not restrict the use of this tasty sauce. Use in any recipe calling for an all purpose tomato sauce. Make lots and lots and freeze in convenient sized containers.

2 onions, chopped
4 large cloves garlic, crushed
2 sticks celery, thinly sliced
a few bay leaves
3 tablespoons olive oil
2 green peppers, seeded and finely chopped

10 large ripe tomatoes, pureed
4 heaped tablespoons tomato paste
2 teaspoons dried marjoram
2 teaspons dried basil
1 teaspoon dried oregano
pinch ground cloves
½ teaspoon salt
1 teaspoon freshly ground black pepper

Saute the onions, garlic and celery with the bay leaves in the olive oil on low heat for 15 minutes.

Add the peppers and continue to saute until the peppers are soft.

Add the tomatoes, the tomato paste, the herbs, cloves and seasoning, and simmer for 20 minutes until the sauce is thick.

SPICED APRICOT SAUCE

1 tablespoon sunflower oil
1 small onion, chopped
1 small clove garlic, crushed
¼ teaspoon cinnamon
¼ teaspoon cardamom
¼ teaspoon cumin
12 fresh apricots, halved
2 tablespoons clear honey

Heat oil in a saucepan. Saute onion and garlic briefly. Add spices, then apricots and honey. Cook gently until a fragrant, golden puree is formed.

NB: keep pan covered. Add a little water if fruit begins to dry.

POLYNESIAN MARINADE

3 tablespoons sunflower oil
1 tablespoon tamari
4 fl oz (100 ml) guava juice
1 teaspoon ground ginger
1 teaspoon cardamom

Mix everything together and use as required for marinating tofu for dishes such as «aloha pizza», «pan Pacific pie» or Polynesian skewers (a variation on «satay kebabs»).

INDONESIAN MARINADE

large knob fresh ginger (about 1 oz /25 gm), grated
½ teaspoon Chinese 5 spice
2 cloves garlic, crushed
3 tablespoons tamari
4 tablespoons walnut oil
1 tablespoon mango chutney
4 tablespoons sherry

Beat everything together, chopping any large lumps in the chutney, or whirl in your processor.

PACIFIC CHILLI SAUCE

Makes about 1½ pints (850 ml).

---

1 large onion, chopped
1 large Bramley apple, chopped
1 large green pepper, chopped
4 cloves garlic, crushed
1 tablespoon thyme
1 teaspoon chilli powder
2 tablespoons sunflower oil

juice of 1 lemon
5 teaspoons coconut cream
3 tablespoons tomato paste
2 tablespoons tamari
1 teaspoon sugar
1 lb (450 gm) tomatoes, chopped

1 slice pineapple, chopped (optional)
1 banana, sliced (optional)

Saute onion, apple, pepper, garlic, thyme and chilli in oil on low heat, until onion is soft.

Add lemon juice and coconut cream, and bring slowly and carefully to the boil. Stir in tomato paste, tamari and sugar, and simmer for 5 minutes. Stir in the tomatoes, and simmer a further 10 minutes. Remove from heat, and cool. Can be fridged or frozen.

Five minutes before needed (after reheating gently, if from cold) add the optional pineapple and banana.

SPICY ALMOND–CHILLI SAUCE

Makes about 1½ pints (850 ml).

1½ onions, chopped
3 cloves garlic, crushed
1 green pepper, chopped
1 red pepper, chopped
1 teaspoon salt
1 teaspoon pepper
sunflower oil

2 tablespoons tahini
3 tablespoons tomato paste

3 tablespoons lemon juice
1 tablespoon cayenne
2 tablespoons chilli powder
1 pint (600 ml) vegetable stock
12 oz (350 gm) toasted almonds, roughly chopped

Saute the onions, garlic, and peppers in sunflower oil, with salt and pepper.

Add tahini, tomato paste, lemon juice, cayenne and chilli powder. Fry quickly for 2 minutes, then slowly stir in the stock. Bring to boil and simmer gently. As it thickens, stir in the almonds. The flavour can be adjusted by adding more seasoning, chilli powder or lemon juice.

FRESH MANGO SAUCE

If you have been marinating tofu, you can use the surplus marinade for this rich Indonesian sauce.

½ quantity «Indonesian marinade»
(or leftover «lumpia» marinade)
1 perfectly ripe fresh mango
tamari

Peel the mango and cut all the flesh away from the stone. Puree with the marinade, and heat gently just to warm through. Adjust seasoning with tamari.

FRESH TOMATO SALSA WITH AVOCADO

3 spring onions, chopped
6 large tomatoes, halved
small handful fresh coriander leaves
small handful fresh parsley
1 teaspoon olive oil
1 tablespoon lime juice
1 large avocado, peeled and stoned
salt and chilli powder or tabasco to taste

Put all ingredients, barring the seasonings, in a food processor, and puree. Season to taste and chill several hours.

PEANUT–CHILLI SAUCE

This simple to make sauce is designed for those who do not like a hot chilli flavour.

1 large onion, chopped
4 large cloves garlic, crushed
2 carrots, chopped
2 celery sticks, chopped
1 inch (2 cm) piece fresh ginger root, grated
1 teaspoon chilli powder
2 tablespoons sunflower oil

7 oz (200 gm) toasted peanuts, chopped
6 good sized tomatoes, pureed
zest and juice of 1 large lemon
9 oz (250 gm) crunchy peanut butter
3 tablespoons tomato paste
3 tablespoons tamari

Saute the first 6 ingredients in the oil until all the vegetables are tender. Take off the heat, and stir in everything else. Taste and check the seasoning.

REFRIED BEANS

Use to fill tortillas, adding grated cheese, chopped fresh vegetables and salsa to taste, or omit the chilli and use, with any of the chilli sauces, in recipes like «papadzules» or «Mexican chilli bake».

2-3 tablespoons olive oil
2 onions, chopped
4 cloves garlic, crushed
1 teaspoon ground cumin
1 teaspoon ground coriander
chilli powder to taste
18 oz (500 gm) cooked red kidney beans

Heat the oil and add the onion, garlic, cumin, coriander and chilli if used. Stir fry 2 minutes. Add the beans and stir until everything is heated through. Mash some of the beans if you wish.

MEGALITHS

Illustrations by Debi Ani

Avebury's largest stone circle is said to have had 99. The West Kennet Avenue may have had as many as 300. But Stones Restaurant's megaliths are infinite! The creative process is always at work and at least one eye-appealing and flavoursome new dish appears on our lunchtime counter every day. In compiling this chapter, we have recreated for you just a fraction of the thousand or more different megaliths savoured by our customers over the past five years.

We chose the particular dishes according to the same criteria we use in the restaurant each day when deciding what to make for lunch. There are bright bakes and steaming golden pies to cheer up cold wet days, light lunches and suppers for summer, warming autumnal casseroles and rich hot pots, and stuffed potatoes to enjoy around the fire on a frosty winter night. Think of the season and the weather when you select a recipe to try.

We have attempted to cover as wide as possible a range of ingredients and ways of combining ingredients. Use the recipes as they stand, then experiment with different vegetables, fruits, nuts, pulses and so on, use lots of different fresh herbs, and try different seasonings. The megalithic avenue really does stretch infinitely into the distance, and only you can map its course.

STEAM, SAUTE OR STIR FRY?

Not so much a recipe, but more a way of life. How often have you been confronted with soggy, overcooked vegetables, or worse still, vegetables left to stand in their own cooking water? The answer (confirmed by a quick poll round our kitchen), is likely to be all too often.

If you have a single vegetable to cook, perhaps as a component in one of the recipes, or as an accompaniment to another dish, steam it. You can use a purpose made steamer for this, or simply put the prepared vegetables into a heavy pan with a tiny amount of water, cover with a tight fitting lid and steam until just *tender and still brightly coloured. Take off the heat* immediately and cool (if for use in a dish) or eat at once. When steaming harder vegetables, such as swedes or parsnips, it helps to add a knob of margarine or butter to the pan. A little drop of milk takes the acid edge off spinach.

The difference between sauteeing and stir frying lies simply in the intensity of heat involved and the amount of 'elbow grease' required! To saute, stir gently over medium heat. To stir fry, frantically turn your vegetables over and over and over on the maximum heat possible. Most vegetables used in our recipes are cooked by one or the other of these methods (you will find the terms used often), but also remember that a combination of sauteed or stir fried vegetables and fruits, served perhaps with rice, makes a superb meal in its own right.

The cooking order is the same for both sauteeing and stir frying. So, for a comprehensive stir fried feast, first assemble your ingredients for a good range of flavours, textures and colours. Next, wash and trim as necessary, then cut into contrasting shapes or leave whole, always bearing in mind the natural form of the fruit or vegetable in your hand. Now, divide your prepared ingredients into cooking order:

HARD (eg onions, garlic, carrots, celery)
MEDIUM (eg broccoli, cauliflower, courgettes, French beans)
SOFT (eg peppers, mushrooms, marinated or smoked tofu, pineapple)
NO COOK (eg shredded Chinese leaves, any sort of sprouted bean or seed)

Heat your chosen oil or oils (select from sunflower, olive, walnut, sesame, coconut) in a wok or very large, heavy based pan on high heat. Add the 'hard' ingredients and any spices you choose (eg Chinese 5 spice, grated fresh ginger, whole coriander, crushed cardamom pods). Stir fry until the onion turns transparent. You may need to throw in a splash of water or fruit juice and tamari to prevent scorching. Now add the 'medium' vegetables and keep stir, stir, stirring until everything is just beginning to soften. Add a splash more liquid if necessary. Take at once off the heat, and add the 'no cook' ingredients. Check and adjust seasoning and serve!

LEEK, MUSHROOM & WHITE WINE GRATIN

For this gratin, choose a cheese with a distinct flavour, such as Lancashire or white Stilton. Serves 6.

6 good sized leeks
1 lb (450 gm) mushrooms, sliced
3 oz (75 gm) butter
4 oz (100 gm) wholewheat flour
¼ pint (150 ml) white wine
1 pint (550 ml) milk
¼ pint (150 ml) cream
handful fresh parsley, chopped
12 oz (350 gm) wholewheat breadcrumbs
12 oz (350 gm) sesame seeds
6 oz (175 gm) cheese, grated
walnut or hazelnut oil to moisten

Clean and slice leeks, and saute in butter with mushrooms. When leeks soften, sprinkle over flour. Cook for 2 minutes, stirring. Pour in wine. Simmer for 5 minutes. Add milk, cream, parsley and seasoning. Carry on cooking for 10 minutes. Transfer to baking dish.

Combine all the topping ingredients, and spread over the leek mixture. Bake at 170° for 45 minutes.

CAULIFLOWER, FENNEL & PINE NUT CROUSTADE

A pale but very interesting dish. The fennel adds depth of flavour to the cream sauce. Serves 6.

2 small cauliflowers, broken into florets
6 small fennel bulbs, chopped
1 onion, chopped
knob of margarine
pinch oregano
1 bay leaf
7 fl oz (200 ml) white wine
½ pint (300 ml) cream
1 tablespoon tamari
pepper
8 oz (225 gm) pine nuts
6 oz (175 gm) breadcrumbs
pinch salt
walnut or sunflower oil to moisten well

Saute cauliflower, fennel and onion in margarine with herbs. Add wine, cover and simmer for 10 minutes.

Add cream, tamari and pepper. Turn into ovenproof dish.

Combine the croustade ingredients (pine nuts, breadcrumbs, salt and oil) and sprinkle over cauliflower mixture. Bake at 160° for 30 minutes, until topping is golden and crisp.

CREAMY SUMMER VEGETABLE BOULANGERE

The message of this dish is the sweet freshness of new summer vegetables. If you're lucky enough to have your own vegetable plot, celebrate with us your fortune! Cut the parsnips artistically to match the carrots in shape and size. You may use half kohlrabi and half potatoes for the topping, instead of just potatoes. Serves 6.

1½ pints (850 ml) vegetable stock
handful fresh thyme and lemon balm, roughly chopped
18 oz (500 gm) garden fresh baby carrots, washed and trimmed
18 oz (500 gm) garden fresh baby parsnips, washed and trimmed
1 large or 2 medium onions, sliced
3 cloves garlic, crushed

3 courgettes, cut into ½ inch (1 cm) slices
11 oz (300 gm) tender young runner beans, sliced diagonally

4 oz (100 gm) margarine
about 2 oz (50 gm) wholewheat flour
milk

zest and juice of 1 large lemon
large handful chopped fresh parsley
1½ lb (750 gm) new potatoes, sliced and steamed till just tender
sunflower oil for brushing
2 tablespoons toasted sesame seeds

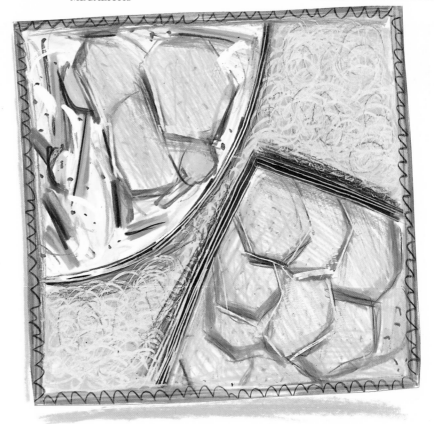

Bring the stock to boiling point with the herbs, and add the carrots, parsnips, onions and garlic. Cover and simmer for 15 minutes.

Add the courgettes and the runner beans, and simmer 5 minutes more, or until everything is crisp tender. Carefully preserving the stock, drain the vegetables and set them aside.

Melt the margarine on low heat, and stir in enough flour to absorb the marg. Cook, stirring, for 1 minute. Make up the reserved stock to 1½ pints (850 ml) with milk, and gradually beat into the roux. Cook gently until a thick and creamy sauce is achieved. Remove from heat.

Stir in the lemon zest and juice, and the parsley. Season with a little salt and generous pepper. Stir in the set aside vegetables. Turn this mixture into a margarined ovenproof dish. Arrange overlapping potato slices on top. Brush with oil and sprinkle with sesame seeds. Bake at 190° for about 35 minutes, or until the top is lightly browned and crisp.

KOULIBIACA

A delicious filling beneath a decorative plait of nutty pastry. Serves 6.

1 quantity «nut pastry» made with pecans
1 oz (25 gm) butter
1 onion, sliced
1 red pepper, cut in strips
2 small fennel bulbs, sliced thinly
4 fl oz (100 ml) white wine
8 oz (225 gm) cream cheese
2 tomatoes, chopped
juice of 2 lemons
12 oz (350 gm) cooked rice
8 oz (225 gm) cooked chickpeas
2 dill pickles, sliced
3 hard boiled eggs, chopped
egg and sesame seeds for decorating pastry

Saute onion, pepper and fennel in butter. When the vegetables soften, add the wine, cover and simmer for 5 minutes.

Mix together cream cheese, tomatoes, lemon juice, rice, chickpeas, pickles and eggs. Add to fennel. Season to taste.

Roll out pastry into a long rectangle. Grease baking sheet. Place pastry over sheet with plenty hanging over the edges. Pile filling into the middle section, in a long heap. Cut the uncovered pastry into inch (2½ cm) wide strips, and fold each strip to the centre of the filling. Tuck in the ends. Brush with egg and scatter seeds. Bake at 180° for 50 minutes.

COURGETTES STUFFED WITH CAERPHILLY & ALMONDS

Hilary first made a similar dish to this while camping on the beach at Paltsi on the Volos peninsula in Greece. She was given a very large courgette by a visitor on a donkey, who indicated his intention of returning for supper. Wild walnuts, almonds and herbs from the valley, feta cheese, yogurt and eggs from the taverna and dried mushrooms and spices from the backpack were stuffed into the courgette shell. The two halves were firmly tied together, wrapped in several layers of foil and baked in the lunchtime fire embers for several hours.

The results were excellent, as was the retzina and strawberry grapes for dessert! The version here is more conveniently cooked in the oven. Serves 6.

3 large courgettes on the way to becoming marrows
2 large cloves garlic, crushed
1 large onion, finely chopped
2 oz (50 gm) margarine
9 oz (250 gm) mushrooms, roughly chopped
7 oz (200 gm) Caerphilly cheese, grated
4 oz (100 gm) breadcrumbs
7 oz (200 gm) ground almonds
handful chopped fresh parsley
1 teaspoon ground cloves
2 eggs
4 fl oz (125 ml) soured cream
4 oz (100 gm) Caerphilly, grated
24 whole almonds

Halve the courgettes lengthwise, and scoop out the middles leaving a thin but strong shell. Chop the removed flesh.

Saute the garlic and onion in the margarine until the onion turns transparent. Add the mushrooms and courgette middles and cook gently, stirring frequently for 5 minutes. Take off the heat.

Stir in the grated cheese, the crumbs, the ground almonds, parsley and cloves, and mix everything very well. Taste and season.

Beat together the eggs and soured cream, and use this to bind the vegetable mix. Pile all the stuffing into the reserved courgette shells and top with the Caerphilly. Decorate with the whole almonds. Arrange the filled courgettes in an attractive greased shallow ovenproof dish, and cover with foil. Bake at 180° for 45 minutes, removing the foil for the last 15 minutes cooking time.

LAMMAS ROAST

Almost unnoticed amongst fifteen other workers and thousands of customers on a typical midsummer weekend, Julia created this very popular roast. Serves 6.

1 onion, chopped
2 cloves garlic, crushed
3 leeks, sliced
½ celery head, sliced
1 lb (450 gm) shelled peas
1 lb (450 gm) wholewheat breadcrumbs
8 oz (225 gm) cheese, grated
1 tablespoon tamari
4 eggs, beaten
7 courgettes, diced
9 tomatoes, chopped
1 large onion, chopped
½ teaspoon each basil and thyme
2 tablespoons olive oil

Start with the roast, and saute the onion, garlic, leeks and celery until they are soft. Stir in the peas, and remove from heat. Add remaining ingredients.

For the filling, saute all the vegetables and herbs in a covered pan until the tomatoes melt to form a thick sauce. Oil a tray or deep metal quiche dish. Press in half the roast mix, spread over the filling, then top with remaining roast. Bake at 170° for 45 minutes.

MUSHROOM & RUNNER BEAN CACCIATORE

Affectionately known by at least one group of our customers as 'Taggers'! You can substitute any other fresh, seasonal green coloured vegetable for the beans, or use a selection of vegetables. Experiment with different cheeses. Serves 6.

9 oz (250 gm) tagliatelli nests
18 oz (500 gm) freshly picked runner beans, sliced
2 medium onions, roughly chopped
9 oz (250 gm) carrots, sliced
3 sticks celery, sliced
3 large cloves garlic, crushed
a few bay leaves
3 tablespoons olive oil

4 fl oz (100 ml) orange juice
4 fl oz (100 ml) water
2 teaspoons vegetable stock concentrate
4½ fl oz (125 ml) medium sherry
2 heaped tablespoons tomato paste
14 oz (400 gm) whole button mushrooms
5 fl oz (150 ml) medium sherry
handful chopped fresh marjoram (or use 1 tablespoon dried)
1 quantity «thick cheese sauce»
2 tablespoons grated Parmesan cheese

Cook the tagliatelli nests to 'al dente', drain and set aside.

Steam the runner beans until just tender (about 7 minutes), and set these aside too.

In a large pan, saute the onion, carrot, celery and garlic with the bay leaves in the oil until everything is crisp tender (except the bay leaves!).

Heat the water and orange juice to just below boiling point and stir in the vege-

table concentrate until it has dissolved. Add this stock to the vegetables, together with the sherry and tomato paste. Simmer for 10 minutes.

Add the mushrooms and the rest of the sherry, and simmer 5 minutes more. Take off the heat and stir in the marjoram, the runner beans and the tagliatelli. Mix everything together well, and season with tamari and plenty of freshly ground black pepper.

Pile into an ovenproof dish, and cover with the cheese sauce. Sprinkle with the Parmesan and bake at 190° for 20 minutes, or until the top is golden and bubbly.

VEGETABLE BOURGUIGNONNE

The joy of this dish is in its slow cooking, allowing the vegetables to absorb the wine and herbs. It could also be cooked in the simmering oven of a solid fuel range for a proportionately longer time. Serves 6.

2 tablespoons sunflower oil
3 courgettes, cut into thick slices
8 oz (225 gm) new carrots
1 lb (450 gm) new potatoes
2 leeks, sliced
12 oz (350 gm) pickling onions or shallots, peeled and whole
1 lb (450 gm) button mushrooms
1 parsnip, sliced
1 head celery, sliced
2 bay leaves

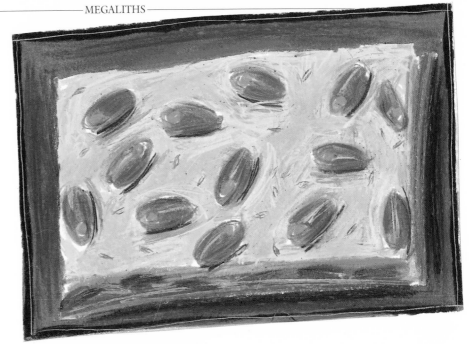

3 tablespoons wholewheat flour
¾ pint (400 ml) red wine
2 tablespoons tomato paste
2 tablespoons lemon juice
1 tablespoon dried sage

12 oz (350 gm) cheese, eg Teifi or white Cheshire, grated

Saute vegetables and bay leaves in oil for 20 minutes. Stir in flour, cook for ½ a minute, then add wine, tomato paste, lemon juice and sage. Cover and either slowly simmer on the top of the stove for 1 hour, or bake in the oven at 150° for 50 minutes, or until vegetables are tender.

If casseroled, scatter cheese over during last 10 minutes. Or if cooked on top of the stove, add the cheese when the bourguignonne is transferred to a serving dish, and melt quickly under a grill.

MASTERPIZZA

We have been making this, and variations, since the restaurant opened, and have always had to move the oven shelves to fit it in! Serves 9-12.

1 prebaked «pizza base»
1¼ pints (¾ l) «pizza sauce»

12 oz (350 gm) cheddar, grated
1 large red and 1 large green pepper, very thinly sliced
12 oz (350 gm) mushrooms, thinly sliced
6 large tomatoes, sliced
14 oz (400 gm) Teifi cheese (or Mozzarella), grated
12 stuffed olives, sliced thinly
1 tablespoon dried oregano
1 tablespoon olive oil

Spread the pizza sauce evenly over the pre-cooked pizza base (still on its tin).

Next, make a perfectly even layer with the cheddar. Arrange the pepper slices in a flat layer over the cheddar. Top the peppers with a flat layer of mushrooms (keep the edges square and the surface flat at all times, otherwise you will have an ovenful of overflowed pizza – we speak with experience). Cover the mushrooms with the sliced tomatoes. Spread the grated Teifi perfectly evenly over the tomatoes, and decorate with the sliced stuffed olives. Sprinkle the oregano over all, and drizzle with the olive oil. Bake at 190° for 40-45 minutes.

CAULIFLOWER & MANGETOUT GRATIN

Using watercress as a herb adds a peppery tang to sauces. Serves 6.

1 oz (25 gm) butter
1 cauliflower, in sprigs
handful mangetout peas
1 onion, sliced

nutmeg, for grating
7 fl oz (200 ml) white wine
4 tablespoons wholewheat flour
7 fl oz (200 ml) cream
7 fl oz (200 ml) milk
2 bunches watercress, chopped
handful fresh parsley, chopped
1 lb (450 gm) cooked beans (flageolet or haricot)

12 oz (350 gm) cheddar, grated
2 oz (50 gm) sesame seeds
4 oz (100 gm) jumbo oats
3 oz (75 gm) rolled oats
olive or walnut oil

Saute vegetables in butter. Generously grate nutmeg over, and pour on wine. Cover and simmer until cauliflower softens a little. Add the flour, and cook briefly. Pour in cream and milk, and season. Stir in chopped cress and parsley. Simmer for 5 minutes. Fold in beans. Check seasoning. Transfer to serving dish.

Thoroughly moisten cheese, oats and seeds with oil. Spread the topping over the cauliflower mix. Bake at 160° for 40 minutes.

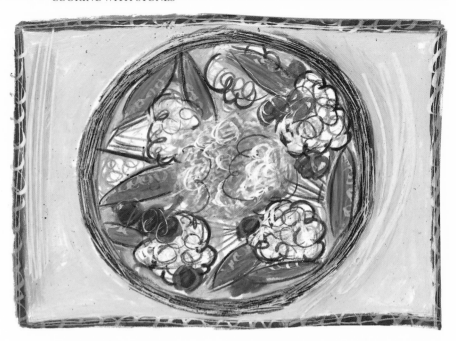

SPINACH, MUSHROOM & NEW POTATO GRATIN

Fresh peas are a luxury food. This dish enhances their special flavour and emerald gleam. Serves 6.

1 oz (25 gm) butter
1 onion, sliced
1 lb (450 gm) mushrooms, sliced
1 lb (450 gm) spinach leaves
7 fl oz (200 ml) white wine
2 lb (900 gm) peas, shelled
15 fl oz (400 ml) single cream
2 tablespoons arrowroot

3 lb (1400 gm) new potatoes, cooked and sliced
2 oz (50 gm) butter
pinch thyme

Melt butter and saute onion. Add mushrooms and spinach, and cook quickly. Add white wine and peas. Simmer for 2 minutes. Pour in cream and arrowroot. When sauce is thickened, pour into ovenproof serving dish.

Top with overlapping potato slices, and dot with butter. Sprinkle thyme and salt and pepper over, and bake at 170° for 50 minutes.

FILLED PROVENCAL TOMATOES

A light, herb filling of wine and mushrooms, with the tang of olives. Serves 6.

6 large beefsteak tomatoes
1 onion, chopped
2 cloves garlic, crushed
9 oz (250 gm) marron mushrooms
2 tablespoons olive oil
a good handful of fresh marjoram, rosemary and thyme, mixed
¼ pint (150 ml) red wine
3 oz (75 gm) stuffed olives
3 eggs, separated
5 oz (150 gm) wholewheat breadcrumbs
5 oz (150 gm) cheddar, grated
5 oz (150 gm) cheddar, sliced

Slice tops off tomatoes, and scoop out insides.

Saute onion, garlic and mushrooms in oil. Add herbs and wine, and cook for 5 minutes.

Transfer to blender and add olives and breadcrumbs. Whizz for 20 seconds. Beat in egg yolks. Whip whites, and fold into mushroom mixture with grated cheese.

Pile mix into tomato shells, arranging them in a greased dish as you fill them. Top with cheese slices and replace lids. Cover with foil and bake at 170° for 40 minutes.

GOOD SHEPHERD PIE

'Good shepherds don't eat sheep ...' The ideal dish to accompany Handel's Messiah. Serves 6.

2 tablespoons sunflower oil
1 onion, chopped
2 carrots, chopped
2 celery sticks, chopped
2 courgettes, chopped
½ teaspoon each thyme and basil
¼ teaspoon celery seed
2 bay leaves
8 oz (225 gm) walnuts
9 tomatoes, chopped
12 oz (350 gm) mushrooms, sliced
¾ pint (425 ml) tomato juice
3 tablespoons tomato paste
8 oz (225 gm) cooked red kidney or aduki beans
2 tablespoons tamari
1 cooking apple, chopped
2 oz (50 gm) margarine
8 allspice berries, crushed
3 lb (1350 gm) well cooked potatoes
3 eggs, beaten
2 oz (50 gm) margarine
walnuts for topping

Saute vegetables in oil with herbs and nuts. Cover and cook until vegetables soften.

Add tomatoes, juice and paste, beans and tamari, and simmer for 20 minutes. Transfer to ovenproof serving dish.

Cook together the apple, 2 oz (50 gm) of margarine and allspice to form a puree. Then mash this with the potatoes, eggs and another 2 oz margarine. Smooth the topping onto the vegetable base, and scatter nuts over. Bake at 180° for 60 minutes.

LASAGNE VERDI WITH POLPETTINI & DEVON OKE

Change the meaning of the word 'lasagne'! Serves 6-8.

Olive oil for brushing dish
16 strips wholewheat lasagne verdi, cooked 'al dente'
⅓ quantity «light white wine tomato sauce»
18 oz (500 gm) Devon Oke cheese, grated
12 «polpettini»
4 eggs
½ pint (300 ml) natural yogurt
handful stuffed olives
handful chopped fresh parsley
2 oz (50 gm) Parmesan cheese, grated
4-6 tomatoes, sliced

Brush a shallow ovenproof serving dish with olive oil. Cover the base of the dish with 6 strips of the lasagne, overlapping if necessary.

Cover with the tomato sauce, and sprinkle with half the Devon Oke. Artfully arrange the polpettini on top of the cheese. Cover with the remaining 6 lasagne strips.

Beat the eggs with the yogurt, and stir in the remaining Devon Oke, the olives and the parsley. Pour this sauce over the lasagne strips.

Decorate with tomato slices, and sprinkle with the Parmesan. Bake at 180° for 35 minutes, until bubbly and golden brown.

POLPETTINI

Hilary first ate polpettini at a wonderful restaurant on a boat in Syracuse harbour (Sicily), whilst working on an excavation on the acropolis at Agrigento. Our version can be served simply with pasta tossed with butter, garlic, Parmesan cheese and parsley, or used in «Lasagne verdi with Devon Oke» or as substitutes for falafel in «Middle Eastern egg rolls». Makes about 20.

2 lb (900 gm) spinach, with large stalks removed
4 oz (100 gm) margarine or butter
1 whole nutmeg, grated

zest of 2 lemons
7 oz (200 gm) wheatgerm
7 oz (200 gm) pine nuts
4½ oz (125 gm) raisins
1 teaspoon salt
generous freshly ground black pepper
4 eggs, beaten

handful of wheatgerm for coating
olive oil for baking

Wash spinach and dry in a salad spinner. Melt margarine/butter in a thick based pan. Stir in spinach and nutmeg, and cook, stirring often, until the spinach has wilted, but still retains its bright green colour. Squeeze out any excess moisture, and puree the spinach in a food processor, or chop it very finely.

Combine the wheatgerm, pine nuts, raisins, lemon zest, salt and pepper in a large bowl. Stir in the spinach and mix thoroughly. Stir in the beaten eggs.

Form the mixture (which will be quite wet) into ping-pong size balls, and roll in wheatgerm. Drizzle each ball with a few drops of olive oil and bake at 170° for about 20 minutes, or until just firm to the touch.

CORNISH LICKY PIE WITH CLOTTED CREAM & CIDER

The inspiration for this dish came from a similarly named creation seen in a shop window in Falmouth. Serves 6.

2 lb (1 kg) leeks, sliced ½ inch (1 cm) thick
7 fl oz (200 ml) cider
4 sprigs fresh sage, finely chopped
(or 1 tablespoon dried sage)
2 tablespoons full strength English coarse grained mustard

4 oz (100 gm) margarine
4 cooking apples, cored and finely sliced
9 oz (250 gm) button mushrooms, sliced
4 tablespoons wholewheat flour
½ pint (300 ml) cider
7 fl oz (200 ml) hot water
1 tablespoon vegetable stock concentrate
1-2 teaspoons apple and sage jelly

18 oz (500 gm) new potatoes, sliced and cooked in vegetable stock
4 tablespoons Cornish clotted cream

1 quantity «basic pastry»

Cook the leeks gently in the cider with the sage, until the leeks are just crisp tender, and the cider has all gone. Remove from heat and stir in the mustard. Set aside.

In another pan, melt the margarine and saute the apples, stirring continuously for 2 minutes. Add the sliced mushrooms and stir to coat with the melted marg. Stir in the flour and stir everything round ½ minute longer. Gradually add the warm stock (made with the cider, water and concentrate) and simmer until the sauce is thick. Take off heat and stir in the apple jelly to taste.

Overlap the potato slices (when cooking these, make sure you stop when they are just tender) on the base of a well greased, deep pie dish. Pour over the apple-mushroom sauce and top with the leeks. Dot with the clotted cream and cover with the pastry. Brush with beaten egg and bake at 160° for 1 hour or until the pastry is golden brown.

RED WINE & NUT ROAST WITH BRIE

Slices of nutty roast, with a softly melting interior. Serves 6.

1 red and 1 green pepper, diced
1 fat clove garlic, crushed
2 large leeks, chopped
3 oz (75 gm) margarine
4 fl oz (100 ml) red wine
4 oz (100 gm) each brazils, cashews and almonds
(all nuts roasted and coarsely ground)
12 oz (350 gm) wholewheat breadcrumbs
handful fresh parsley, chopped
3 leaves fresh sage, chopped
5 eggs, beaten
tomato juice to moisten
8 oz (225 gm) Sharpham Brie, sliced

Saute pepper, garlic and leeks in margarine for 10 minutes, add wine and simmer for another 5 minutes. Stir in nuts, crumbs and herbs. Remove from heat, beat in the eggs, adding tomato juice to make a soft but not runny mixture.

Oil a deep, circular iron flan dish. Spread in half the roast mix, over which you arrange the slices of Brie and top with remaining roast. Bake at 170° for 45 minutes.

CAULIFLOWER & COURGETTE POLONAISE

A creamy cauliflower nestling into a bright vegetable filled sauce. Serves 6.

1 handsome cauliflower
1 bay leaf
1 tablespoon tamari
3 tablespoons olive oil
5 courgettes, sliced
1 onion, sliced
1 teaspoon each savory and tarragon
6 large mushrooms, sliced
½ oz (15 gm) arrowroot
5 tomatoes, chopped
6 oz (175 gm) wholewheat breadcrumbs
4 hard boiled eggs, chopped
2 oz (50 gm) fresh parsley, chopped
2 oz (50 gm) butter/margarine, softened

Heat in a pan enough water to half submerge the cauliflower. Bring to the boil with the bay leaf and tamari. Cook for 10 minutes, covered. Remove from liquid and put to one side, reserving the liquid.

Heat olive oil in saucepan. Add onion and courgettes and cook with herbs and seasonings until onion softens. Add mushrooms and ¼ pint (150 ml) liquid reserved from cauliflower.

Slake arrowroot with a little cold water, and add to courgette mixture. Stir until thickened. Check seasoning. Add chopped tomatoes, and simmer for 5 minutes.

Transfer this mixture to ovenproof serving dish, and place cauliflower on top. Prepare polonaise topping by mixing together the dry ingredients (breadcrumbs, chopped egg and parsley) and season with pepper. Gently mash with the butter or margarine. Spread this liberally over the cauliflower, and bake at 180° for 45 minutes.

111

MIDDLE EASTERN EGG ROLLS

Mrs Beeton knew them as aubergines, but English gardening books were still calling them eggplants at least up until the First War, as, of course, they have always been known across the Atlantic. In this recipe, long slices of eggplant are rolled around Egyptian style falafel: egg rolls from the Middle East.

To make Mediterranean egg rolls, increase the garlic, substitue a mixture of cheddar and Parmesan for the fetta, and use «polpettini» instead of falafel. Serve this with buttered and parsleyed shell pasta.

Serves 6.

2 large, firm aubergines of cylindrical properties *olive oil for baking*
9 oz (250 gm) spinach, washed and thoroughly spun dry *2 oz (50 gm) margarine* *2 eggs* *1 small nutmeg, grated* *2 handfuls chopped fresh parsley* *2 oz (50 gm) wheatgerm* *9 oz (250 gm) feta cheese* *9 oz (250 gm) cottage cheese* *1 large clove garlic, crushed* *½ teaspoon salt* *pinch pepper*
about a dozen «falafel» (one for each roll)

Take the aubergines, and cut off the ends – the stems from the tops, and thin slices from the rounded bottoms. Stand the trimmed fruits upright, and cut very carefully, lengthwise, into ¼ inch (½ cm) thick slices. Discard the first and last slices (too much skin), and you should be left with a total of 12-14 good sized slabs. Liberally oil enough baking sheets to lay out the aubergine slices. Brush the topsides with more olive oil, and bake at 160° for 15-20 minutes until the slices are soft but not mushy. Set aside.

Next make the filling. Melt the margarine and saute the spinach, until just wilted. Puree with the egg and nutmeg. Turn this mixture into a bowl, and stir in the parsley and the wheatgerm. Puree together the cheeses, garlic and seasonings, and add to the spinach mixture.

Spread the filling evenly over the baked aubergine slices and place a falafel in the centre of each. Curl the slices around the falafel and secure each with a toothpick. Stand the finished egg rolls upright in a liberally olive oiled, attractive shallow ovenproof dish and cover loosely with foil. Bake at 180° for about 35 minutes, or until everything is heated through. Serve with green beans in a light tomato sauce, or with grilled tomatoes and a salad.

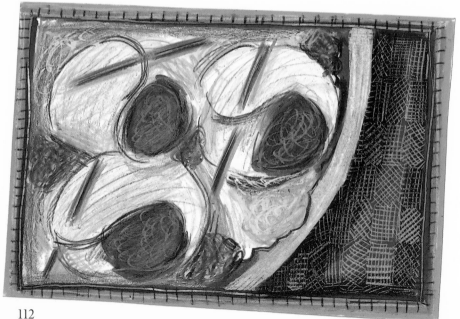

SOUFFLE STUFFED JACKETS

We never present simple jacket potatoes in the restaurant. Instead, we take the idea a stage further by baking the potatoes, hollowing them out and filling the shells with lots of different delicious mixtures. Try any of the pancake fillings, or «Boston baked beans» topped with cheese, «refried beans» mixed with «peanut-chilli sauce» and topped with soured cream, or this tangy souffle mix, first served in winter 1987. Serves 4.

2 large baking potatoes, baked until tender
2 tablespoons «lemon-herb-garlic mayonnaise»
4 tablespoons cottage cheese
2 teaspoons dried dill weed
4 oz (100 gm) sharp cheddar, grated
pinch chilli powder
pinch salt
2 teaspoons full strength English coarse grain mustard
small handful chopped fresh parsley
2 eggs, separated
1 large tomato cut into eight

Cut the potatoes in half, lengthwise, and with a sharp edged spoon, carefully remove the middles into a bowl, leaving a ¼ inch (½ cm) shell. Set the jackets aside.

Mash the middles, and add the mayonnaise, the cottage cheese, the dill, three quarters of the cheddar, the seasonings, mustard and parsley. Mix well, then beat in the egg yolks. Fold in the stiffly beaten egg whites. Pile the filling back into the jackets and sprinkle with the remaining grated cheese. Decorate with the tomato. Bake in a lightly oiled baking dish at 170° for about 25 minutes, until puffy and golden. Serve with salads or steamed vegetables.

113

BOSTON BAKED BEANS

'Boston baked beans' because the recipe was invented by Hilary in her original Boston bean pot. For a Canadian flavour, substitute maple syrup for the molasses. These beans keep well in the fridge, and are happily reheated for several dishes, so if you are particularly partial to baked beans, make a double quantity! Serves 4-6.

9 oz (250 gm) haricot or blackeyed beans
3 tablespoons molasses
5 tablespoons tomato paste
2 tablespoons demerara sugar
1 tablespoon tamari
2 tablespoons red wine vinegar
½ teaspoon pepper
1 tablespoon dried savory
1 small onion, finely chopped
7 fl oz (200 ml) water

Pre-soak and boil the beans until tender.

Mix all the seasonings and the onion and water together in a bowl, and stir in the drained beans. Transfer to an attractive ovenproof casserole with a tight fitting lid. Use foil if necessary to ensure a perfect seal. Bake at 130° for at least 3 hours. Serve with «Stilton and herb muffins» or on toast topped with cheese. These beans also make a delicious filling for baked potatoes.

WALNUT & PECAN ROAST

Serves 6.

sunflower oil
1 large onion, chopped finely
2 sticks celery, sliced
2 large carrots, chopped finely
7 oz (200 gm) wholewheat breadcrumbs
5 oz (150 gm) pecans, chopped
5 oz (150 gm) walnuts, chopped
big handful of chopped fresh parsley
4 fl oz (100 ml) natural yogurt
2 eggs, beaten
1½ lb (700 gm) spinach
nutmeg for grating
3 oz (75 gm) Devon Oke cheese, grated

Heat oil and cook onion until tender, add celery and carrots and cook for about 10 minutes. Remove from heat and add breadcrumbs, nuts and parsley. In a bowl combine the yogurt and eggs, then transfer to nut mixture.

Wash spinach, remove large stalks, shake off excess water, then cook for about 10 minutes in the moisture still clinging to the leaves, with a generous grating of nutmeg. Remove from heat, drain any excess liquid and stir in cheese.

Grease a 7 inch square tin (18 x 18 cm) and arrange a few pecans on the base in a pattern. Place half the nut mixture in the tin, then spinach, then remaining nut mixture. Cook at 170° for 1 hour, under foil for the first ½ hour. Turn out onto a plate proud enough to carry a walnut and pecan roast with style, and serve with an appropriate sauce.

NOAH'S RAINBOW PIE

Who needs a pot of gold when you can have a pie like this? Noah sometimes likes chopped sauteed spinach as a change from broccoli. Serves 8.

1 oz (25 gm) margarine
8 oz (225 gm) carrots, grated
4 tablespoons (60 ml) lemon juice
1 tablespoon clear honey
8 oz (225 gm) mushrooms, thinly sliced
1 clove garlic, crushed
knob margarine
1 teaspoon lemon juice
12 fl oz (375 ml) cottage cheese
12 fl oz (375 ml) «more than basic tomato sauce»
3-4 potatoes, sliced and steamed until just tender
14 oz (400 gm) broccoli florets, steamed for 5 minutes
½ teaspoon grated nutmeg
8 oz (225 gm) tomatoes, thinly sliced
1 teaspoon dried basil
1 teaspoon dill weed
Red Leicester cheese, grated
2 lb (900 gm) «basic pastry»
egg and sesame seeds for decorating pastry

Melt the margarine on low heat, and stir in the carrots and lemon juice. Cook, covered, for 10 minutes. Take off the heat and stir in the honey. Set aside.

Saute the mushroom slices and garlic gently in the margarine for 2 minutes, then take off the heat, sprinkle with the lemon juice and set aside.

Measure out the sauce and the cottage cheese, separately of course. Your rainbow is now taking shape.

Season the sliced cooked potatoes, and set them aside in a separate container.

Stir the grated nutmeg into the steamed broccoli and put this beside the rest of the prepared ingredients.

Sprinkle the sliced tomatoes with the herbs, and set them aside. Measure out the quantity of Red Leicester cheese.

Oil a deep baking dish, and line with slightly less than half the pastry. You are now completely ready to assemble Noah's pie. Simply layer up the prepared ingredients in the lined dish in the following order: carrot, mushrooms, cottage cheese, tomato sauce, potatoes, broccoli, tomatoes, Red Leicester cheese. Cover with the pastry lid, and use any left over pastry to make a rainbow for decoration. Brush the finished pie with beaten egg, and sprinkle with sesame seeds. Bake at 180° for 45 minutes.

MOUSSAKA WITH ALMONDS

Evocative of the 'wine dark sea' and Aegean islands. You could vary this recipe by substituting hazel nuts for almonds, or using a different cheese, such as Red Leicester, and making the cheese sauce with yogurt in place of milk. Serves 6.

2 tablespoons olive oil
1 large onion, chopped
3 small bay leaves
1 heaped teaspoon each thyme and marjoram
2 green and 2 red peppers, sliced medium thick
2 cloves garlic, crushed
1 large aubergine, diced
2 large courgettes, diced
8 fresh tomatoes, chopped
½ pint (300 ml) tomato juice

3 tablespoons olive oil
pinches of thyme and marjoram
1 large aubergine, sliced

8 oz (225 gm) whole toasted almonds
4 large potatoes, par-cooked and sliced

3 eggs
«thick cheese sauce»
2 oz (50 gm) flaked almonds

Saute onion in olive oil with herbs, and cook until onion turns transparent. Mix peppers, garlic, aubergine and courgettes into onion, and cook until peppers soften (add a little extra oil if needed). Add tomatoes and juice, and simmer until all vegetables are tender. Check seasoning.

In a fresh pan, heat olive oil with a pinch each of the herbs. Add some of the aubergine slices, and fry in the oil (add more oil if needed). Remove cooked aubergine, then repeat oil, herbs and aubergine until all the slices have been sauteed just soft.

Layer in a dish aubergine, courgette and pepper mix; toasted almonds; potato slices; slices of sauteed aubergine.

Beat 3 eggs into a cheese sauce made with a full-flavoured English cheese such as a sharp cheddar or Devon Oke, and pour over aubergine slices.

Scatter flaked almonds on top. Bake at 175° for 40 minutes, until golden.

ASPARAGUS SOUFFLE OMELETTE

Joe, now 81, comes to Stones for lunch with his wife Joan at precisely 12.15 every Wednesday. For two years, under doctor's orders, he was allowed neither wheat nor dairy products, although he could eat eggs. We made this simple but perfect dish for him with the first asparagus of 1986. You can vary the filling according to what is seasonally available. Serves 1.

6 stalks tender asparagus, trimmed
2 oz (50 gm) dairy free margarine
juice of ½ lemon
3 eggs, separated
2 tablespoons water
pinch each salt and pepper
knob of margarine for frying
zest of ½ lemon

Steam the asparagus until just tender. Toss with the melted margarine and lemon juice and keep warm.

Beat the egg yolks with the water until thick and creamy. In a separate bowl, beat the egg whites with the salt and pepper, until they stand up in peaks when the whisk is withdrawn. Gently fold the whites into the yolks.

Melt the extra knob of margarine on medium to high heat until foaming, then pour in the egg mixture. Cook for 2-3 minutes, loosening the edges with a palette knife, until the bottom surface is firm and golden. Lay the lemony asparagus in the centre of the omelette, and fold in half. Sprinkle with the lemon zest, and serve immediately on a hot plate with grilled tomatoes and saute potatoes.

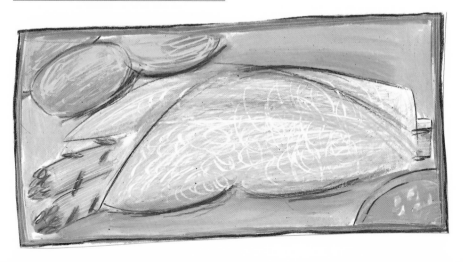

NEAPOLITAN AUBERGINE WITH SHELL PASTA

Any of the smaller pasta shapes can be used here – wheels, bows, etc. Serves 6.

8 oz (225 gm) pasta shells, cooked in lightly salted water
2 onions, sliced
2 fat cloves garlic, sliced
3 red peppers, sliced
4 tablespoons olive oil
2 aubergines, diced and salted
2 bay leaves.
1 teaspoon thyme
1 teaspoon marjoram
6 courgettes, sliced
12 tomatoes, chopped
3 tablespoons tomato paste
6 oz (175 gm) farm cheese (eg Teifi or Lancashire), grated
14 oz (400 gm) wholewheat breadcrumbs
sunflower oil to moisten

Prepare pasta shells.

Saute onion, garlic and peppers in oil. Add aubergines, bay leaves and herbs. Finally add courgettes, tomatoes and paste. Cover and simmer for 20 minutes, until sauce thickens. Fold in the pasta shells. Pour into ovenproof dish.

Combine cheese, breadcrumbs and oil to make the gratin top, and sprinkle over the aubergine mix. Bake at 180° for 50 minutes.

GADO GADO

This pan-Indonesian dish, featuring both stir fried and raw fruits and vegetables, looks and tastes spectacular. Vary the ingredients according to the season, always bearing in mind the balance of tastes, textures and shapes. Serves 8.

1 quantity «peanut chilli sauce» (mild or spicy)
about 4 lb (1800 gm) of seasonal vegetables, such as: *carrots, cut into batons* *celery, in diagonal slices* *onions, cut into rings* *courgettes, in batons* *broccoli, in bite sized florets* *baby corn, whole or split* *white cabbage, coarsely shredded*

3-4 tablespoons sesame or sunflower oil splash of tamari
2 large handfuls of fresh bean, chickpea or lentil sprouts *2 tablespoons sunflower seeds* *2 tablespoons toasted cashew pieces* *4 eggs, hard boiled and sliced* *½ block smoked tofu, cut into thin slices* *3 interesting looking hard dessert apples, cored and wedged* *1 orange or 2 mandarins, peeled and segmented* *2 small limes, sliced*

Warm the peanut chilli sauce, gently. At the same time, warm a big and beautiful serving dish.

Stir fry the vegetables in the oil in normal order, until everything is just right. Remove from heat, and season with tamari. Quickly turn half the vegetables into the warmed dish, cover with all the chilli sauce and then the remaining vegetables.

Sprinkle with the sprouts, seeds and nuts. Now think Indonesian (smile!), and decorate with the eggs, tofu and fruit. Serve immediately.

CAULIFLOWER, WHITE WINE & PINE NUTS

The pine nuts add to the creamy taste and texture. Serves 6.

3 oz (75 gm) margarine *1 onion, chopped* *1 clove garlic, crushed* *1 red peper, diced* *¼ pint (150 ml) dry white wine*
1 medium cauliflower
2½ oz (75 gm) wholewheat flour *1 pint (550 ml) milk* *1 bay leaf* *1 mace blade*
1½ lb (700 gm) potatoes, cooked and sliced *5 oz (150 gm) pine nuts* *8 oz (225 gm) Devon Oke cheese* *2 oz (50 gm) fresh parsley, finely chopped*

Melt margarine and saute onion and garlic. Add pepper, and cook until onion softens. Add wine and fast simmer for 5 minutes.

Break cauliflower into florets, and steam until the point of a knife meets scant resistance.

Add flour to wine and onion mixture, and stir for 1 minute. Heat milk briefly with bay leaf and mace, and add gradually to the sauce. Simmer for 5 minutes, stirring frequently. Add seasoning, and taste.

Gently fold cauliflower into sauce. In greased dish, layer from bottom upwards:

half the potato slices
cauliflower mix
half the pine nuts
half the cheese
the rest of the potato slices
the remaining cheese, pine nuts
and parsley.
Bake at 170° for 50 minutes.

FLAGEOLET, MUSHROOM & MANGETOUT STROGANOFF

Fresh French tarragon is good if you can find it (is there anyone out there growing it?!). Serves 6.

1 large onion, chopped
large pinch tarragon
2 oz (50 gm) margarine
12 oz (350 gm) whole mushrooms
2 tablespoons tamari
2 oz (50 gm) wholewheat flour
1 pint (550 ml) milk
3 generous tablespoons soured cream
1 lb (450 gm) cooked flageolet beans
1 lb (450 gm) mangetouts, steamed but still
crisp and bright green

Cook onion and tarragon in margarine. Add mushrooms and tamari, cook briefly and add flour. Stir well and gradually pour in milk, followed by soured cream, beans and mangetouts. Simmer gently for 15 minutes, stirring frequently. Taste and season.

SWISS VEGETABLE PIE

A savoury dish inspired by the Swiss breakfast combination of apples and yogurt. Serves 6.

1 head celery, cut into strips
1 small cauliflower, in florets
3 red peppers, in strips
3 large courgettes, in strips
knob butter
2 tablespoons coarse-grained mustard
¾ pint (400 ml) natural yogurt
8 oz (225 gm) cheddar, grated

1 lb (450 gm) carrots, grated
1 lb (450 gm) potatoes, grated
2 eating apples (eg Discovery), grated
2 tablespoons sunflower oil
pinch salt

Saute vegetables in butter until softening. Add mustard, yogurt and cheese. Stir togther over low heat. Turn into baking dish.

Mix grated vegetables and apples together with oil and salt. Press onto the vegetable and yogurt mixture. Cover with oiled foil and bake at 170° for 40 minutes. Remove foil, and continue to bake until topping crisps and browns.

CELERY, CASHEW & ALMOND ROAST

This roast with its stuffing of tomatoes and Red Leicester cheese, looks beautiful when cut, and tastes even better! It can be made at any time of year, so is suitable for any celebration. Use fresh thyme in summer. Serves 6-8.

2 oz (50 gm) margarine
2 large onions, finely chopped
3 large cloves garlic, crushed
1 whole large celery head, trimmed and finely sliced
½ pint (300 ml) water
2 teaspoons vegetable stock concentrate
handful chopped fresh thyme (or 1 tablespoon dried)
handful chopped fresh parsley
zest and juice of 2 lemons
9 oz (250 gm) ground almonds
5 oz (150 gm) chopped cashews
4 oz (100 gm) porridge oats
3 eggs, beaten

5 oz (150 gm) Red Leicester cheese, grated
4 large tomatoes, sliced
additional tomato slices to decorate

Melt margarine and saute onions, garlic and celery for 5 minutes. Blend the water and stock concentrate, add to pan and simmer 5 minutes more. Take off heat and stir in the herbs, lemon juice and zest. Cool slightly and stir in the nuts and oats (reserve a little of the nuts for topping). Season to taste, and bind with the beaten eggs.

Spread half of the roast mixture into a well margarined ovenproof dish. Cover with the grated cheese and then with the tomato slices. Top with the remaining nut mixture, and decorate with the extra tomato slices. Bake, covered with foil, at 160° for 45 minutes. Remove the foil and bake for 10 minutes longer.

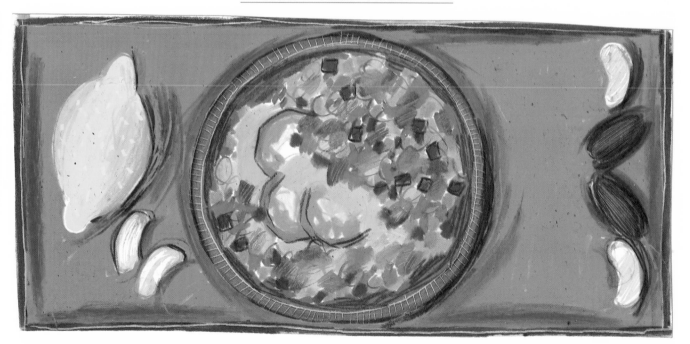

PANCAKES

Pancakes are fun to make (except on hot days!), and are always very popular for lunch at Stones. In all the pancake batter recipes, the amount of liquid required may vary according to the absorbency of your particular flour. Try a little less than stated, and if, after standing, the mixture seems too thick (it should be like double cream), beat in a little extra water. Vary your basic pancakes with different flours and liquids, and try adding chopped fresh herbs, spices, ground nuts and toasted seeds to the batters.

As we always bake our pancakes in foiled trays of 6 or 7, rather than attempting individual instantly filled crepes (we can have upwards of 400 people for lunch ...), we choose moist fillings, and usually serve with a friendly sauce. The following recipes are intended as inspiration for experimenting. The fillings, which are favourites at Stones, are also delicious for scooped out jacket potatoes or other hollowed vegetables.

WHOLEWHEAT PANCAKE BATTER

You can enliven this basic wholewheat recipe by adding chopped fresh herbs or ground spices to the mix, after everything is beaten in. Makes 6 x 8 inch pancakes, with a little to spare in case of tossing error!

4½ oz (125 gm) wholewheat flour
1 teaspoon salt
2 large eggs
¼ pint (150 ml) milk
4 fl oz (100 ml) water
sunflower oil for frying

Combine the flour and salt, and beat in the eggs with a little of the milk. Gradually add the rest of the milk and the water, beating all the time. Put the mixture in the fridge, and let stand half an hour.

Have ready by your stove a frying slice, an upturned dinner plate and a heat proof jug of sunflower oil. At the end of the standing time, beat the batter once more and add more liquid if needed. With the hotplate on high, heat 1-2 teaspoons of the oil in your favourite pancake pan, swirling the pan round and round so all the base is thinly coated in oil. Pour any excess back into your oil jug.

When the oil is just smoking, pour 3-4 tablespoons of the batter (you'll have to guess this!) into the pan and swish it quickly to form a neat pancake shaped circle. Cook for about 30 seconds, constantly loosening the edges with your slice and shaking the pan. When the pancake is entirely free, turn with the slice or toss. Cook 15-20 seconds on the other side, then slide immediately onto your upturned plate. Repeat the process with the rest of the mixture, and fill as soon as possible after cooking.

ULTRALITE WHOLEWHEAT PANCAKE BATTER

These are ideal for subtle fillings such as oyster mushrooms or sauteed asparagus or as dessert pancakes filled with fresh fruit and natural yogurt or fromage frais. Makes 6.

5 oz (150 gm) wholewheat flour
1 teaspoon salt
3 eggs
3 tablespoons (50 ml) milk
7 fl oz (200 ml) water

Follow the method for «wholewheat pancake batter».

GRAM PANCAKE BATTER

This is a recipe we use for our several customers requiring a gluten-free meal. You will note that there is also no milk. Makes 6.

5 oz (150 gm) gram flour
1 teaspoon salt
3 eggs
7 fl oz (200 ml) water

Follow the method for «wholewheat pancake batter».

BUCKWHEAT PANCAKE BATTER

Good filled with «ratatouille» or any spicy, robust mixture. Makes 6.

3 oz (75 gm) buckwheat flour
3 oz (75 gm) wholewheat flour
1 teaspoon salt
3 eggs
¼ pint (150 ml) milk
7 fl oz (200 ml) water

Follow the method for «wholewheat pancake batter».

TOMATO PANCAKE BATTER

Tomato pancakes marry perfectly with spinach or cream cheese based fillings. Makes 6.

4½ oz (125 gm) wholewheat flour
1 teaspoon salt
pinch chilli powder
2 eggs
2 tablespoons tomato paste
4 fl oz (100 ml) tomato juice
¼ pint (150 ml) water

Mix together the flour, salt and chilli powder and beat in the eggs with the tomato paste. Gradually add the tomato juice and water. Let stand as for «wholewheat pancake batter».

Follow the method for «wholewheat pancake batter». If you use the fresh coriander, add it when the batter is complete and stir very well before cooking to distribute the herbs.

FLORENTINE PANCAKE BATTER

Use a tomato filling, perhaps with cream cheese, in these speckly green pancakes, or try a rich dark mushroomy mixture and top with a light tomato sauce. Makes 6.

9 oz (250 gm) spinach, washed and shaken dry
3½ fl oz (100 ml) water
4½ oz (125 gm) wholewheat flour
1 teaspoon salt
½ teaspoon mace
3 eggs
7 fl oz (200 ml) milk

Cook the spinach on high heat with only the water clinging to the leaves, until it has wilted and all the moisture has evaporated. Take off the heat and puree with the measured water.

Combine the flour, salt and mace, and beat in the eggs and milk. Gradually add the spinach puree. Beat well and leave to stand 30 minutes. Beat again before cooking.

QUICK TORTILLAS

Fill with «refried beans», cheese and chopped raw vegetables, or use in «Mexican chilli bake» or for «papadzules». Makes 6.

3 oz (75 gm) maize meal
2 oz (50 gm) wholewheat flour
1 teaspoon salt
2 eggs
7 fl oz (200 ml) water
a few sprigs of fresh coriander, chopped (optional)

MARRON, CHEESE, PARSLEY & ALMOND PANCAKES

After you have filled your 6 pancakes and popped them in the oven, warm any left over filling with a little milk and yogurt, add more parsley and some red pepper strips, and use as a sauce.

6 «wholewheat pancakes» or «tomato pancakes»
1 oz (25 gm) butter
14 oz (400 gm) marron mushrooms, thickly sliced
2 eggs, beaten
7 fl oz (200 ml) milk
½ pint (300 ml) natural yogurt
½ nutmeg, grated
pinch salt
½ teaspoon pepper
4½ oz (125 gm) whole almonds, coarsely chopped
4 oz (100 gm) ground almonds
7 oz (200 gm) cheddar, grated
2 oz (50 gm) Parmesan cheese, grated
lots and lots of chopped fresh parsley
sunflower oil for baking

Melt the butter on low heat and stir in the marrons. Saute gently for 5 minutes, stirring often. Take off the heat and set aside.

Beat the eggs with the milk, yogurt and seasonings. Stir in the nuts and cheeses, then the parsley. Finally, stir in the marrons and check the seasonings.

Pack the filling into the pancake skins of your choice and roll up. Lay the filled pancakes side by side in a well oiled oblong baking dish. Brush the tops with oil, cover with foil and bake at 180° for about 25 minutes.

FLORENTINE PANCAKES

This filling is superb in tomato pancakes. The recipe makes more than enough for your 6 pancakes, but it is so delicious that it is worth making the larger quantity and inviting more guests to dinner or using the leftovers to top grilled tomatoes or flat field mushrooms.

---

6 «tomato pancakes»
2 small onions, chopped
3 large cloves garlic, crushed
2 oz (50 gm) margarine
3 tablespoons wholewheat flour
½ pint (300 ml) natural yogurt
4 fl oz (100 ml) milk
4 fl oz (100 ml) white wine
11 oz (300 gm) tight button mushrooms, sliced thin
4 oz (100 gm) blue cheese, grated or crumbled
5 oz (150 gm) mild cheese (eg Caerphilly or Wensleydale) grated

---

18 oz (500 gm) just picked spinach, washed and spun dry
3 eggs
9 oz (250 gm) cottage cheese
1 teaspoon ground mace
½ teaspoon salt
½ teaspoon pepper

Saute the onions and garlic in the margarine. Stir in the flour and cook, stirring, for 30 seconds. Gradually add the yogurt, milk and wine, and cook gently until a thick smooth sauce is obtained. Take off heat. Stir in the mushrooms, the blue cheese and the Caerphilly or Wensleydale. Set this mixture aside.

Cook the spinach, stirring all the time, in only the water clinging to the leaves (adding a few drops if it sticks) until it is just wilting. Remove from heat and puree with the eggs. In a separate bowl, beat the cottage cheese with the seasonings and stir in the pureed spinach. Fold the cottage cheese-spinach mixture into the mushroom sauce. Fill, roll and bake the pancakes as usual.

RED CABBAGE, CIDER & SULTANA PANCAKES

The bright yellow of the pancakes, the rich reds of the cabbage and apples and the strong autumny flavours are reminiscent of Vermont in the fall.

6 «gram pancakes»
1 small firm red cabbage, weighing 1½ lb or so (750 gm)
1 large onion, chopped
1 tablespoon sunflower oil
½ teaspoon cinnamon
2 teaspoons caraway seeds
7 fl oz (200 ml) cider vinegar
4½ oz (125 gm) sultanas
3 gaily coloured dessert apples, cored and thinly sliced
small handful chopped parsley
soured cream to serve

First prepare the cabbage. Cut it in half from top to toe, and cut out all the white stalky part. Thinly slice what is left, again from top to toe.

Saute the onion in oil until transparent. Add the spices and cabbage, and cook, stirring, 1 minute more. Add the vinegar and sultanas. Turn down the heat and simmer, covered, for 30 minutes. Add the apples, and cook a further 5 minutes, stirring now and then. Take off heat, season and add the parsley. Cool and refrigerate as long as possible in a covered container, for the flavours to develop.

Fill, roll and bake the pancakes as usual, putting any spare filling along the edge of the baking dish. Serve the heated pancakes with a generous blob of soured cream.

OYSTER MUSHROOM & RUNNER BEAN PANCAKES

A simple but elegant filling for a special occasion. You can substitute mangetout peas for the runner beans.

6 «ultralite wholewheat pancakes»
14 oz (400 gm) freshly picked tender runner beans
½ teaspoon salt
½ teaspoon pepper
1 oz (25 gm) butter
18 oz (500 gm) oyster mushrooms, trimmed
2 teaspoons lemon juice
pinch of salt
sunflower oil for baking
1 quantity «Brie and red pepper sauce»

Slice the beans diagonally, steam until crisp tender and cool quickly in a strainer under cold running water. Sprinkle with salt and pepper and set aside.

Melt the butter and stir in the mushrooms, very gently so as not to break the shapes. Stir just to coat with the butter then take off the heat and sprinkle with lemon juice and salt.

Very carefully mix the beans and mushrooms together and fill the pancakes, arranging any unused filling along the edge of the dish. Brush with oil, cover with foil and reheat for 10-15 minutes only. Serve with «Brie and red pepper sauce».

MUSHROOM STUFFED CABBAGE

Seems like a lot of mushrooms, but it needs very little accompaniment. Good as an impressive centre dish (dairy and gluten free). Serves 6.

8 oz (225 gm) butter or margarine
3 onions, finely chopped
2½ lb (1150 gm) marron or field mushrooms, finely chopped
1 lb (450 gm) parsnips, diced
12 oz (350 gm) ground pecans
2 tablespoons tamari
2 tablespoons tahini
1 well formed green cabbage
a few crushed juniper berries

Melt half the butter or margarine and saute onions and mushrooms, covered, for 20 minutes. Cook diced parsnips in remaining butter, then mash and combine with mushroom mix, along with nuts, tamari and tahini. Set aside to cool.

Take your cabbage, and remove any outer leaves that are damaged. Cut a deep cross through to near the bottom. Heat a roomy pan of water with a dash of tamari to simmering point. Plunge cabbage in, cover and cook gently for 20 minutes. Remove and drain. Place in a round buttered dish. The cabbage will fall open. Spread mushroom mixture between the leaves, and scatter over juniper berries. Cover with foil and bake at 180° for 1 hour.

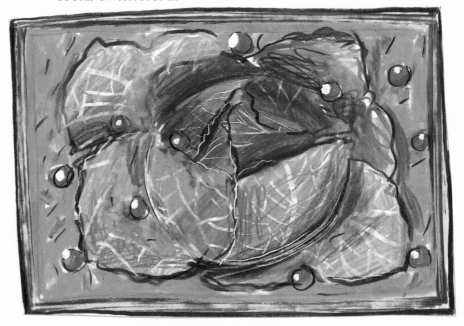

ALOHA PIZZA

What could be more logical than a Pacific variation on an old Italian theme (to a Stones arrangement)? Serves 9-12.

1 block fresh tofu
1 quantity «Polynesian marinade»
1 prebaked «pizza base»
1¼ pints (¾ l) «Pacific chilli sauce»
12 oz (350 gm) cheddar, grated
2 peppers, sliced thinly
12 oz (350 gm) mushrooms, sliced
1 mango, peeled and sliced
1 large banana, thinly sliced
12 oz (350 gm) Teifi cheese, grated
1 avocado, peeled and sliced
a 3 inch (8 cm) slice from a small pineapple, thinly sliced

Press the tofu, and marinate overnight if possible.

Spread the pizza base with the chilli sauce. Carefully cover with the cheddar, keeping the thickness even. Arrange an even layer of peppers over the cheese, and a layer of mushrooms over the peppers. Remove the tofu from the marinade, and lay this over the mushrooms. Keep the edges square and the surface flat at all times: heed the caution in the «Master-pizza» recipe!

Next make a layer of mango and banana slices. Cover with the Teifi, and decorate with the avocado and pineapple. Bake at 200° for 25-30 minutes.

128

PAPADZULES

'Hay comida sin carne?' is not the most popular request in most Mexican restaurants. After seemingly endless plain tortillas and not-too-exciting refried beans, with the occasional bowl of fiery guacamole, we discovered papadzules in a large (and largely empty) restaurant in Campeche. These papadzules were not too exciting either, but the idea was born. Serves 6.

6 «quick tortillas»
½ pint (300 ml) «peanut chilli sauce»
8 oz (225 gm) grated cheddar
12 oz (350 gm) just cooked potatoes, cubed
1 small green pepper, cut in strips
1 small red pepper, in strips
4 hard boiled eggs, coarsely chopped
1 avocado, sliced
8 oz (225 gm) «refried beans»
sunflower oil for dish and brushing

Make the tortillas, and spread each with the chilli sauce.

Reserve half the cheese, and divide the remaining ingredients into six equal heaps. Use each heap to fill a tortilla, pack tightly and roll firmly.

Arrange the papadzules (for that is what they now are) in an oiled dish and brush their tops with oil. Sprinkle with the rest of the cheese, cover with foil and bake at 175° for 20 minutes. Remove foil and bake uncovered for a further 5-10 minutes, until everything is heated through and the cheese has melted.

Serve with «fresh tomato salsa», extra peanut chilli sauce and soured cream.

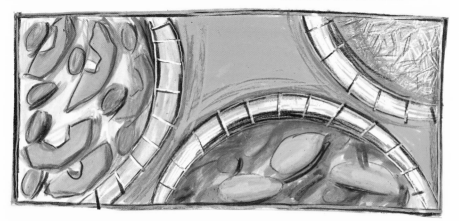

MEXICAN CHILLI BAKE

Serve this as an exciting alternative to the more conventional chilli sin carne, tacos or enchiladas. A different range of flavours and textures with every mouthful! Serves 6-8.

1 quantity «quick tortillas», fried and cut into 2 inch (5cm) strips
1½ pints (850 ml) «spicy peanut chilli sauce»
½ quantity «refried beans»
olive oil for dish

7 oz (200 gm) sharp cheddar, grated
9 oz (250 gm) button mushrooms, thinly sliced
1 green and 1 red pepper, cut into thin strips
5 tomatoes, sliced
9 oz (250 gm) Mozzarella or Teifi cheese, grated

1 ripe avocado
splash of lemon juice
2 tablespoons shelled pistachio nuts
soured cream to taste

Oil a deep baking dish and cover the base with half the tortilla strips, overlapping slightly. Next spread all the peanut chilli sauce over the tortillas and cover with the refried beans. Save any left over beans for a quick chilli supper, or freeze for later use.

Sprinkle the cheddar over the beans. Now make a layer of mushrooms and peppers, and arrange the tomato slices over this layer. Cover with the remaining tortilla strips. Sprinkle the Teifi or Mozzarella over all.

Peel and quarter the avocado, and remove the stone. Cut the flesh into moon shaped slices, sprinkle with lemon juice and arrange interestingly over the cheese. Finish with an extravagant scatter of pistachios. Bake at 175° for 1 hour or until it looks delicious. Serve at once with soured cream.

SPANISH GYPSY CASSEROLE

Serve with pasta or rice and lots of Rioja. Serves 6.

1 large onion, chopped
3 courgettes, halved and sliced
1 head celery, sliced
1 yellow and 2 green peppers, sliced
handful mangetout peas or runner beans
3 tablespoons olive oil
3 cloves garlic, crushed
1 teaspoon paprika
1 tablespoon turmeric
2 bay leaves
1 teaspoon basil

10 fresh apricots, halved
10 tomatoes, chopped
½ pint (300 ml) tomato juice
1 lb (450 gm) cooked chickpeas
pinch cayenne
1 tablespoon tamari

Saute vegetables in oil and garlic over low heat. Add the first set of spices and herbs, and cook for 10 minutes until onion turns transparent.

Add apricots, tomatoes and juice, and chickpeas. Cover and simmer until tomatoes melt into a sauce. Add cayenne, tamari, and seasonings, and taste.

LUMPIA WITH FRESH MANGO SAUCE

Evokes memories of Harry Chew's in Ubud, where the best lumpia ('tampa daging') in Bali are served. Makes 6.

---

4 oz (100 gm) firm fresh tofu, pressed and cubed
3 tablespoons tamari
1 tablespoon sesame oil
½ teaspoon ground cardamom
½ tablespoon grated fresh ginger

4½ oz (125 gm) wholewheat flour
1 teaspoon ground cardamom
½ teaspoon ground ginger
1 teaspoon cumin seed
1 teaspoon salt
4 eggs
¼ pint (150 ml) cold water
sesame oil for frying

---

2 tablespoons sesame oil
½ tablespoon grated fresh ginger
1 large onion, sliced
5 large cloves garlic, crushed
1 small celery head (about 6 sticks), sliced diagonally
2 large carrots, sliced about ¼ inch (½ cm) thick
½ lb (250 gm) French beans, topped and tailed
½ lb (250 gm) cauliflower, in small florets
1 red pepper, cut into strips

---

more sesame oil for greasing dish and brushing
«fresh mango sauce»

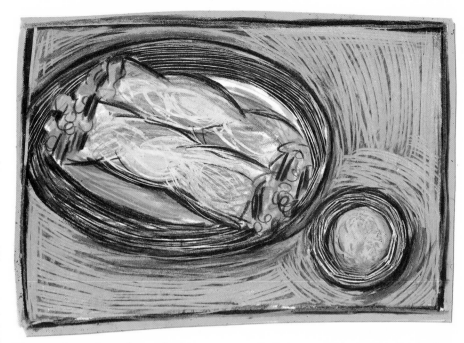

First marinate the tofu, preferably overnight, in the mixed tamari, oil, cardamom and ginger.

Next, the lumpia. Mix the dry ingredients (flour, spices, salt) in a bowl and beat in eggs until thoroughly combined. Gradually beat in all the water. Leave mixture to stand, for at least half an hour. Beat again before making pancakes in the usual way, to distribute spices evenly. The mix should make 6 lumpia, with a little left for good measure. Cook in sesame oil.

Use sesame oil for the stir fry, too. Heat oil in wok, until just starting to smoke. Throw in ginger, garlic, onion, carrot and celery, and stir frantically for about 3-5 minutes, until the onion is just turning transparent. Add the cauliflower and the beans, and continue the frantic stirring,

until all the vegetables are just beginning to be tender. Add the pepper and stir fry 1 minute more. Stir in the drained tofu (reserve the marinade for sauce), and take off heat.

Divide the stir fry between the 6 lumpia, filling each as full as possible. Roll and arrange seamside down in a well oiled ovenproof serving dish (reserve any left over filling for garnish). Brush the filled lumpia with oil, cover with foil and bake at 200° for 20-30 minutes, until heated through. When out of oven, pour fresh mango sauce along middle of dish, and garnish edges with remaining stir fry mixture.

Serve with extra mango sauce and plain steamed rice or «nasi goreng», and much pride.

131

AUTUMN ROOTS & ALE CRUMBLE

Early autumn heralds the return of root vegetables. Pulled when small, they are sweet and crisp. New carrots can be used whole; otherwise, halve any bigger than your little finger. Serves 6.

4 purple kohlrabi, cut into sticks
2 swedes, in sticks
4 turnips, in sticks
bunch new carrots
1 onion, chopped
4 English dessert apples (eg Cox, Discovery or Russet)
2 tablespoons olive oil
large knob butter
sprig of rosemary
sprig of sage

1 bottle (275 ml) dark, strong ale
½ pint (300 ml) vegetable stock
2 tablespoons arrowroot
1 tablespoon tamari

8 oz (225 gm) rolled oats
2 oz (50 gm) jumbo oats
3 oz (75 gm) pumpkin seeds
2 oz (50 gm) sunflower seeds
6 oz (175 gm) Red Leicester cheese, grated
zest of 1 orange
6 oz (175 gm) margarine

Saute the vegetables and apple in oil and butter, turning well. Add sprigs of herbs, cover and cook for 20 minutes.

Add ale and stock and fast simmer for 7 minutes. Stir in slaked arrowroot. Cook until sauce thickens. Stir in jelly and tamari. Check seasoning. Transfer to an ovenproof serving dish.

To make crumble topping, combine dry ingredients, cheese and zest and mix well. Rub margarine in until mixture is a good, crumbly texture. Spread evenly over vegetable base and bake at 170° until topping is a deep golden brown (about 50 minutes).

MARROWBOAT SURPRISE

Nutty, fruity, yummy. Serves 6.

1 medium marrow
1 large onion, sliced
1 red pepper, sliced
3 sticks celery, sliced
3 tablespoons walnut oil
8 oz (225 gm) dried apricots, sliced
7 fl oz (200 ml) white wine

8 oz (225 gm) smoked tofu, cut into small cubes
4 oz (100 gm) broken walnuts
3 oz (75 gm) pumpkin seeds
3 sprigs fresh mint, chopped
2 tablespoons tamari
12 oz (350 gm) cooked rice

12 oz (350 gm) cheese (eg cheddar, Double Gloucester), grated
vegetable stock or white wine to moisten

Halve the marrow, and remove seeds.

Saute vegetables in oil. Add apricots and wine. Simmer, covered, for 10 minutes.

Add tofu, nuts and seeds, then mint, tamari and seasoning. Finally, stir in rice.

Mix well and pack filling into marrow shells. Top with cheese, and bake in a deep dish with a little stock or wine at 180° for 60 minutes.

CURRIED AUTUMN VEGETABLE PIE WITH CAERPHILLY

Large runner beans can be used in this dish. It is better if the vegetable mix is left in the fridge overnight for the flavours to mature. Add the sultanas if a sweeter curry is preferred. It can be reheated, but is also good eaten cold. Serves 6-8.

3 large onions, sliced
4 large cloves garlic, crushed
generous quantity sunflower or sesame oil
1 teaspoon white mustard seeds
1 tablespoon cumin seeds
2 teaspoons coriander seeds
2 teaspoons ground turmeric
2 teaspoons fenugreek
2 teaspoons ground ginger

18 oz carrots (500 gm), in ½ inch (1 cm) slices
18 oz (500 gm) parsnips, sliced as carrots
18 oz (500 gm) kohlrabi, sliced as carrots
1½ pints (850 ml) stock
4 courgettes, in 1 inch (2 cm) slices
18 oz (500 gm) runner beans, cut diagonally

4½ oz (125 gm) creamed coconut, grated
½ pint (300 ml) hot water
10 firm tomatoes, quartered
7 oz (200 gm) sultanas (optional)

7 oz (200 gm) Caerphilly cheese, grated
1½ quantity «basic pastry»
egg for brushing

Saute the onions and garlic in oil for 3 minutes. Add the spices, and stir until the mustard seeds 'pop'. Add the carrots, parsnips, and kohlrabi with the stock, and simmer, covered, for 10 minutes. Add the courgettes and the beans and continue simmering on very low heat, until everything is tender.

Blend the creamed coconut with the water, and add to the vegetable mix. Add the tomatoes (and sultanas, if used), and simmer 5 minutes longer. Take off heat and cool.

When completely cold, turn into a deep pie dish. Sprinkle with the cheese and cover with pastry. Brush with beaten egg and bake at 180° for 1 hour, until golden brown.

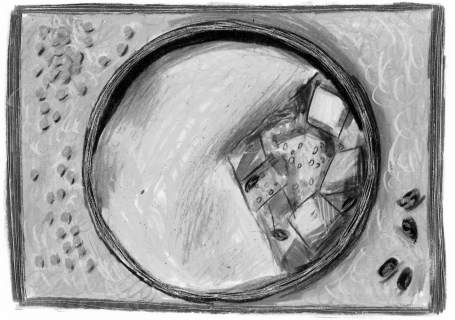

Heat oils in saucepan. Saute onion, garlic and courgettes. Add spices and cook for 1 minute. Stir in lentils and coat in spice and oil.

Make stock with water and concentrate, and add to pan. Simmer until a thick puree is produced (if needed, add a little extra stock). Add tomatoes, tomato paste and raisins, and leave to stand for 12 hours.

Make cheese sauce with the margarine, flour, milk, cheese and flavourings.

Saute onion and carrot in oil until just tender.

In oiled baking dish, layer half lentil mixture; onion and carrot; sliced tomatoes; remaining lentil mixture; cheese sauce. Sprinkle with cayenne and cheddar. Bake at 170° for 60 minutes.

DAHL & SPICED VEGETABLE LAYER

A good way of introducing children to mild Indian spices. Serves 6.

3 tablespoons sunflower oil
1 tablespoon coconut oil
1 large onion, sliced
3 cloves garlic, crushed
4 courgettes, diced
1 pinch ground cardamom
1 tablespoon rhogan josh
1 teaspoon turmeric
1 lb (450 gm) orange lentils

3 pints (1700 ml) hot water
3 teaspoons vegetable stock concentrate
5 tomatoes, chopped
1 tablespoon tomato paste
4 oz (100 gm) raisins

1½ oz (40 gm) margarine
1½ oz (40 gm) wholewheat flour
1 pint (550 ml) milk (cow or soya)
8 oz (225 gm) sharp cheddar, grated
1 pinch mustard
1 pinch cayenne
1 teaspoon tamari

3 tablespoons sunflower oil
1 large onion, sliced
3 carrots, sliced

5 tomatoes, sliced
pinch cayenne
2 oz (50 gm) cheddar, grated

WELSH HOT POT

A hearty winter meal for a crowd. You can vary the vegetables according to what is available in your garden or at the market. Serves 10-12.

4 tablespoons orange zest
1 large onion, sliced
2 tablespoons dried thyme
6-8 potatoes, sliced
3 large spinach or Swiss chard leaves, chopped
1 teaspoon dried savory
1 very small swede, peeled and sliced
1 very small, tightly packed cauliflower, in florets
1 green pepper, cut into strips
4½ oz (125 gm) chopped brazil nuts
3 tablespoons pine nuts
1 tablespoon dried rosemary
3 small parsnips, sliced
4 carrots, sliced
1 red pepper, cut into strips
1 large handful chopped fresh parsley
pepper
2 tablespoons vegetable concentrate
½ pint (300 ml) freshly squeezed orange juice
½ pint (300 ml) water
9 oz (250 gm) Teifi cheese, grated

First, thoroughly margarine a 6-8 pint (3½-4½ l) ovenproof casserole, then assemble and prepare all your ingredients, and lay them out on your worktop in separate heaps. All slices should be about ¼ inch (½ cm) thick.

This casserole has 4 distinct layers, and a hat:

1. Potato and Swiss chard. Line the bottom of the dish with overlapping potato slices (use slightly less than half your potatoes) and the chopped leaves. Sprinkle with 1 tablespoon of the orange zest and all the savory.

2. Swede and onion. Next, layer over-lapping slices of swede, and half the onion. Another tablespoon of orange zest and 2 teaspoons of the thyme will help give this layer its character.

3. Cauliflower and pepper. The third layer consists of the cauliflower, green pepper, nuts, 1 tablespoon orange zest and all the rosemary.

4. Parsnip, carrot and red pepper. Finally, layer overlapping slices of parsnip, red pepper and carrot, the rest of the onion, and scatter over the parsley, a table-spoon of thyme and the last of the orange zest.

5. The hat. Cover everything with the remaining potato slices, and sprinkle generously with pepper.

Make up the stock with the concen-trate, orange juice and water, and pour over. Cover the casserole tightly with foil, then with a good fitting lid. Bake at 150° for 2 hours. Remove the lid and the foil, and sprinkle the cheese all over. Return to the oven for 15-20 minutes, until the cheese is melted and bubbling.

AUBERGINE, COURGETTE & WALNUT CRUMBLE

Other nuts are just as good: try toasted peanuts, hazels, pecans or a combination. Serves 6.

3 tablespoons sunflower oil
2 red onions, sliced
1 clove garlic
8 courgettes, in half-moon chunks
2 aubergines, chunked
1 teaspoon rosemary
1 handful fresh dill weed (or 1 teaspoon dried)
8 allspice berries, crushed

10 tomatoes, chopped
2 large tablespoons tomato paste
1/2 pint (300 ml) tomato juice
1/2 pint (300 ml) vegetable stock

8 oz (225 gm) margarine
12 oz (350 gm) wholewheat flour
8 oz (225 gm) walnuts, ground
8 oz (225 gm) walnuts, roughly chopped
pinch salt

Heat oil and saute onion and garlic. As onion turns transparent, add courgette and aubergine, herbs and spices. Saute briefly.

Add tomatoes, tomato paste and juice and vegetable stock. Simmer until vegetables are tender. Put into oiled baking dish.

To make topping, rub margarine into flour and ground walnuts, then add chopped nuts and salt. Sprinkle evenly over vegetables. Bake at 160° for 45 minutes.

SWEET & SOUR COURGETTE WITH BRAZIL NUT CROUSTADE

A satisfying mingling of flavours. Serves 6.

3 tablespoons sunflower oil
2 onions, chopped
2 cloves garlic, crushed
1 red and 1 green pepper, cut into thin strips
6 stalks celery, cut into 1 1/2 inch (3 cm) sticks
6 courgettes, cut as celery

3 tablespoons arrowroot
3/4 pint (425 ml) pineapple juice
4 tablespoons tomato paste
5 tablespoons red wine or cider vinegar
3 tablespoons lemon juice
4 tablespoons sherry
1 tablespoon basil

9 oz (250 gm) wholewheat breadcrumbs
9 oz (250 gm) broken brazil nuts
3 tablespoons sunflower oil

In a saucepan, saute onions and garlic in the oil. Add the celery and pepper and cook for about 5 minutes. Add the courgettes to this mixture, and stir for a few minutes on a low heat until they are lightly cooked. Remove from heat.

Combine arrowroot and pineapple juice in a jug. Place the tomato paste, vinegar, lemon juice, sherry and basil in a small pan and heat gently, slowly adding the arrowroot solution. Stir until the sauce thickens. Taste and season. Add the sauce to the vegetables and place in an ovenproof serving dish.

Blend breadcrumbs, brazil nuts and oil and spread over the top. Bake at 180° for 35 to 40 minutes, until bubbly around the edge.

PARSNIP & HAZELNUT PIE

If you make this with organicly grown new parsnips and potatoes, and fresh cob nuts, it will be stunning. Also good as a side dish with a roast or savoury bake. Serves 6.

2 large knobs butter
1 onion
5 parsnips, sliced
¼ pint (150 ml) cream
¼ pint (150 ml) natural yogurt
1 tablespoon tamari

2 lb (900 gm) cooked potatoes, sliced
12 oz (350 gm) hazelnuts, roasted
extra butter for topping

Heat butter and saute onion, then parsnips. As they soften add cream and yogurt and tamari. Carry on cooking until tender.

Place a layer of potato on the bottom of a deep dish, then half parsnip mixture, more potatoes, rest of parsnips, then hazel-nuts and finally potatoes. Dot with butter. Bake at 180° for 40 minutes.

PAN PACIFIC PIE

Here is another opportunity for exotic experimentation. Substitute or add grated jicama, steamed chayote slices, grated or thinly sliced fresh coconut, rambutan or mangosteen sections, papaya slices or whatever Pacific produce appears in your market. Serves 6-8.

1 quantity «Indonesian marinade»
1 block firm fresh tofu, pressed and cut into ¼ inch (½ cm) strips
3 tablespoons sunflower oil
2 sweet potatoes, sliced and boiled until just cooked
1 pint (550 ml) «spicy peanut chilli sauce»
½ quantity «refried beans»
4½ oz (125 gm) baby corn, steamed for 3 minutes
1 small green pepper, thinly sliced
1 inch (2 cm) slice off a small pineapple, in slivers
1 large firm banana, sliced as thinly as possible
14 oz (400 gm) mild cheese, grated
1 small mango, sliced neatly
1 avocado, cut into moons

Marinate the tofu several hours or overnight, turning at least twice.

Liberally oil a deep and attractive baking dish, and arrange sweet potato slices in a layer over the base. Combine the peanut chilli sauce and the refried beans, and pour over the potatoes. Next arrange the baby corn and pepper on the sauce. Follow with a layer of pineapple and banana slivers.

Remove the tofu from the marinade (saving the liquid for another purpose), and lay the tofu slices on top of the fruit. Cover with any remaining sweet potato slices, and top with the cheese. Decorate with the mango and avocado, and bake at 180° for 45 minutes.

LEEK & LENTIL LASAGNE

A good dish for serving to a hungry group of friends. Serves 6.

16 sheets lasagne, cooked and cooled
1½ pints (850 ml) «thick cheese sauce», with a generous dash of dry sherry
8 leeks, cleaned and sliced
4 carrots, cut into julienne sticks
4 courgettes, in julienne sticks
2 tablespoons sunflower oil
1½ lb (700 gm) cooked green lentils
8 oz (225 gm) peas, shelled
4 oz (100 gm) toasted hazelnuts
4 eggs
a little extra grated cheese for topping

Prepare lasagne and cheese sauce, and set aside.

Saute leeks, carrots and courgettes in oil. Add lentils, peas and seasoning. Cover and cook gently for 20 minutes. Add nuts.

Beat the eggs into the cheese sauce.

Layer sheets of lasagne with lentil and leek mix, finishing with lasagne. Pour over sauce, and scatter cheese. Bake at 180° for 50 minutes.

IMAM BAYILDI

You too will faint at the taste of these aubergines! In Turkey imam bayildi are all too often seen floating in a puddle of luke warm grease. Not so our version. Serves 6.

3 plump aubergines
1 large onion, chopped
2 courgettes, chopped
1 red and 1 green pepper, chopped
2 fat garlic cloves, crushed
4 tablespoons olive oil
2 bay leaves
1 tablespoon marjoram
1 tablespoon basil
½ tablespoon cumin
½ tablespoon cardamom
6 oz (175 gm) toasted almonds, roughly chopped
juice of 1 lemon
8 oz (225 gm) lexia raisins
7 fl oz (200 ml) red wine
1½ lb (700 gm) cooked rice
1 lb (450 gm) strong cheddar, grated
6 tomatoes, sliced

Halve aubergines lengthwise, and scoop out middles with a soupspoon. Roughly chop the removed flesh.

Saute vegetables and chopped aubergine in oil with bay leaves. When onion softens, add the rest of the herbs and spices, cover, and continue cooking until aubergine is soft. Remove from heat.

Add nuts, lemon juice, fruit, wine, rice and cheese (reserving a little for topping), and mix well. Check seasoning.

Pile mix into aubergine shells. Decorate with tomato slices and remaining cheese. Bake at 180° for 1 hour, covered with foil.

CREAMY ROOTS & SPINACH PIE

Where summer meets autumn. First roots – last leaves. Serves 6.

2 large knobs margarine
2 onions, sliced
4 leeks, sliced
1 head celery, sliced
4 parsnips, sliced
bunch new carrrots, sliced
1½ lb (700 gm) spinach, sliced
bouquet of chopped fresh herbs, eg dill, chives, thyme and mint
handful cherry tomatoes
handful French beans
¾ pint (400 ml) single cream
1 large spoonful thick double cream
1½ quantity «nut pastry»
egg for brushing

Saute first 5 vegetables in margarine until onion softens, then add spinach and herbs, followed by tomatoes and beans, and finally the cream and seasonings. Stir for 10 minutes.

Turn into a pie dish. Decorate with pastry strips, and brush them with egg. Bake at 160° for 1 hour.

FLAGEOLET, MARROW & MUSHROOM PIE

More interesting ways with a marrow. This pie calls for strongly flavoured mushrooms, such as marrons or field varieties. Serves 6.

> *1 large onion*
> *2 yellow or red peppers, sliced*
> *1 medium marrow, in cubes*
> *knob margarine*
> *4 sage leaves, chopped*
> *1 lb (450 gm) tomatoes, chopped*
> *2 cloves garlic, crushed*
> *1½ lb (700 gm) mushrooms, halved*
> *generous dash cider*
> *2 bay leaves*
> *½ pint (300 ml) cream*
> *salt, pepper and tamari*
> *1 tablespoon coarse grained mustard*
> *2 tablespoons arrowroot*
> *1 lb (450 gm) cooked flageolet beans*
> *1 quantity «nut pastry» made with pecans or walnuts*
> *egg for brushing*

Saute onion, pepper and marrow in margarine with sage. When the onion softens, add tomato and garlic, then mushrooms. Add cider and bay leaves. Cover and simmer for 15 minutes.

Stir in cream, seasonings and mustard. When well mixed, add arrowroot and stir until thickening. Fold in flageolets.

Turn into a generous sized pie dish. Top with pastry, and brush with egg. Bake at 160° for 40 minutes.

FILLED ACORN/ SPAGHETTI SQUASH

Any type of squash, marrow or pumpkin can be successfully stuffed with this recipe. Serves 6.

> *3 acorn or spaghetti squash*
> *1 orange and 1 yellow pepper, chopped*
> *1 clove garlic, crushed*
> *2 tablespoons olive oil*
> *pinch marjoram*
> *4 oz (100 gm) currants, soaked in 7 fl oz (200 ml) red wine*
> *small handful arame*
> *large handful of fresh parsley and dill, chopped*
> *8 hard boiled eggs, chopped*
> *12 oz (350 gm) Red Leicester cheese, grated*
> *12 oz (350 gm) cooked rice*
> *4 oz (115 gm) cooked wild rice*
> *sesame seeds and stuffed olives for decoration*

Halve and de-seed squash. Grease baking sheets, and arrange the squash cut side down. Cook at 150° for 20 minutes, until flesh softens. Set aside.

Saute pepper and garlic in oil, with marjoram, for 15 minutes. Add currants, wine and arame and simmer for 10 minutes.

In a roomy bowl, combine all remaining ingredients together with pepper mix. Pack into squash. Decorate with sesame seeds and stuffed olives. Bake at 170° for 45 minutes.

BROCCOLI, MUSHROOM & WALNUT CRUMBLE

Fruit and herb jellies make a sauce sweet and mellow. Redcurrant has an affinity with walnuts. Serves 6.

1 large onion, chopped
1 fat clove garlic, chopped
4 eating apples (eg Discovery), cored and sliced
large knob margarine

2 oz (50 gm) margarine
2 tablespoons wholewheat flour
1 pint (550 ml) milk
dash of cream
1 tablespoon tamari
2 tablespoons redcurrant jelly
6 oz (175 gm) ground walnuts

1½ lb (700 gm) mushrooms, halved

6 oz (175 gm) walnuts, roughly chopped
pinch thyme
small handful rolled oats
2 oz (50 gm) margarine

1½ lb (700 gm) steamed broccoli spears

Saute onion, garlic and apple in margarine until soft.

Start the sauce by making a roux with the margarine, flour and milk, then adding the cream, tamari and redcurrant jelly. Simmer for 5 minutes. Stir in the ground walnuts and check seasoning.

Saute mushrooms and add to sauce.

To make the crumble topping, combine the chopped walnuts, thyme and oats, and rub in the margarine.

Finally, assemble your crumble. Spread onion and apple onto base of circular deep dish. Arrange broccoli spears on top. Pour over mushroom and walnut sauce. Top with crumble mix. Bake at 170° for 45 minutes, until top is crisp and golden.

MARROW & HARICOT CASSEROLE

For when your courgettes go barmy.
Serves 6.

1 small, green, thin-skinned marrow
1 large onion, sliced
1 head celery, sliced
2 oz (50 gm) margarine
3 fresh sage leaves, sliced thinly
2 oz (50 gm) wholewheat flour
¼ pint (150 ml) white wine
1 pint (550 ml) milk
1 tablespoon dry mustard
pinch cayenne
12 oz (350 gm) cheddar, grated
1 lb (450 gm) cooked haricot beans
8 oz (225 gm) cherry tomatoes
1 lemon for squeezing

First halve your marrow, de-seed it and cut into thin crescents.

Saute onion and celery in margarine. Add sage and marrow slices.

When onion softens, stir in flour, then wine, milk, mustard and cayenne. Stir over heat for 10 minutes.

Add cheese, beans and tomatoes, and continue cooking for another 10 minutes. Squeeze lemon juice into casserole, season and taste.

SUMMER FRUIT CURRY

Serve hot, warm or iced. This creamy, spiced sauce with fruits is delicious as an Indian meal with sambals and rice. Serves 6.

2 tablespoons coconut oil
2 cloves garlic, crushed
1 small red onion, thinly sliced
1 small white onion, thinly sliced
1 small red pepper, diced
1 cauliflower, in sprigs
2 pinches each of ground cardamom, turmeric, coriander (preferably fresh), rhogan josh
7 fl oz (200 ml) pineapple juice
1 tablespoon soured cream
15 fl oz (400 ml) single cream
3 tablespoons tomato juice
juice of 2 limes and 2 oranges
2 tablespoons arrowroot

1 small ripe melon, cut into cubes
1 small ripe pineapple, cubed
8 oz (225 gm) green grapes, halved and de-pipped
1 fresh mango, cut into strips
small handful flaked almonds

Heat oil in pan. Saute onion and garlic for 5 minutes, stirring to prevent any scorching. Add red pepper and cauliflower. Add spices and cook for 2 minutes. Add pineapple juice, cover and steam for 10 minutes.

Pour in creams and fruit juices (tomato, lime and orange). Slake arrowroot with a little cold water and add. Heat very gently and stir until sauce thickens.

Add prepared fruits and almonds. Taste and adjust seasoning as necessary (an extra squeeze of lime or pinch of chilli?). Continue to heat gently for 20 minutes.

AUBERGINE KORMA

This casserole is best made a day before needed to let the flavours mingle, and gently reheated on the stove before serving with rice or Indian bread. Serves 6.

3 cloves garlic, crushed
1 large onion, sliced
1 large aubergine, cut into chunks
3 courgettes, sliced thickly
4 carrots, sliced thickly
4 small potatoes, cut into chunks
1 red, 1 green and 1 yellow pepper, cut into chunks
3 tablespoons sunflower oil

2 tablespoons turmeric
½ teaspoon chilli
2 tablespoons cumin seed
2 tablespoons rhogan josh
2 tablespoons ground cardamom

3 bay leaves
2 tins (800 gm each) Italian tomatoes
½ pint (300 ml) tomato juice
4 oz (100 gm) creamed coconut
salt

Saute all vegetables in oil, except tomatoes.

When onion softens, add all spices and cook, stirring, for 5 minutes.

Add bay leaves, tomatoes and juice. Simmer, covered, for 45 minutes. Add coconut and salt. Cook for another 30 minutes at a low simmer. Test potato and aubergine pieces for doneness and check for strength of spices and seasoning.

CHEESE & VEGETABLE PIE WITH FRESH DILL

The nuts in the pastry can be toasted hazels or pecans. Serves 6.

1½ quantity «nut pastry»
3 oz (75 gm) margarine
3 medium onions
1 lb (450 gm) diced carrots
8 oz (225 gm) French beans, cooked
8 oz (225 gm) broccoli, cooked
handful fresh dill, chopped

4 eggs
7 fl oz (200 ml) single cream
8 oz (225 gm) grated cheese

8 tomatoes, sliced
sesame seeds

Line a greased dish with half of the pastry.

In a saucepan, saute onions and carrots in margarine until soft. Stir in beans, broccoli and dill.

Beat eggs with cream and seasonings, and stir in cheese. Mix well into vegetables.

Pour into pastry case, arrange tomato slices over vegetables and cover with pastry lid. Brush with egg, sprinkle over sesame seeds, and bake at 160° for 50 minutes.

143

SOUR CREAM & ONION PIE

Also good with a Sage Derby cheese or Devon Garland – a creamy, semi-hard cheese with a pale green middle layer of chopped herbs. Serves 6.

1½ quantity «nut pastry»
2 large onions, thinly sliced
3 oz (75 gm) margarine
1 teaspoon salt
1 teaspoon dry mustard
3 tablespoons lemon juice
1 tablespoon wholewheat flour
2 eggs, separated
3½ fl oz (100 ml) single cream
3½ fl oz (100 ml) natural yogurt
(or 7 fl oz/200 ml soured cream)
4 oz (100 gm) cheddar, grated
3 hard boiled eggs, sliced
sesame seeds for decorating pastry

Line pie dish with half pastry.

Saute onion in margarine with salt until soft. Add mustard, lemon juice and flour. Cook for 5 minutes.

Combine beaten egg yolks, cream and yogurt (or soured cream) and cheese. Stir into onion mix and simmer for 10 minutes, stirring. Whip whites and fold into sauce. Pour into pastry case.

Arrange egg slices over top. Put on pastry lid. Brush with egg, decorate with pastry leaves and sesame seeds. Bake at 160° for 50 minutes.

MEAL IN A JACKET

Left over vegetables are fine for this dish. But make sure the herbs are fresh: marjoram, lovage and parsley are nice. A quick supper dish for 4, or 2 very hungry people.

4 large baking potatoes, baked until tender
1 onion, chopped
1 tablespoon sunflower oil
2-3 handfuls steamed or stir fried vegetables
4 fl oz (125 ml) soured cream
4 fl oz (125 ml) natural yogurt
4 eggs, beaten
small handful chopped mixed herbs
2 teaspoons tamari
½ teaspoon pepper
12 oz (350 gm) subtle farm cheese (eg Caerphilly), cubed

Halve the potatoes, and scoop out the middles into a large bowl, leaving a strong but not thick shell. Arrange the shells in a lightly oiled, ovenproof dish ready for filling.

Saute the onion in oil until transparent, then mix with the cooked vegetables. Mash the potato middles and beat in the soured cream, yogurt, eggs, herbs and seasonings. GENTLY stir in the onion-vegetable mixture and the cubed cheese. Pile all into the potato shells and bake at 170° for 30-35 minutes, until golden brown. Serve with a crisp green salad.

TIGER PIE

The tiger's stripes are made with alternate layers of brightly coloured ingredients. He is trapped inside by the pastry top, but you can hint at the danger beneath by making artistic use of any left over pastry! Serves 6.

1 quantity «basic pastry», made entirely with wholewheat flour
2 large onions, sliced *4 sticks celery, sliced* *2 fat cloves garlic, crushed* *1 tablespoon sunflower oil* *3 oz (75 gm) pecans, coarsely chopped*
8 oz (225 gm) flat mushrooms, sliced *sprig thyme* *knob margarine* *4 oz (100 gm) rolled oats* *5 oz (150 gm) Red Leicester cheese, grated*
2 large carrots, grated *1 tablespoon sunflower oil* *pinch caraway seed* *2 oranges, peeled and segmented* *1 teaspoon apple jelly*
6 oz (175 gm) cooked aduki beans *1 large swede* *2 tablespoons tahini*
3 parsnips, thinly sliced *1 tablespoon maple syrup* *knob butter*

There are five vegetable mixes to prepare, which you need to keep in separate dishes before making the pastry. Leave seasoning until all five are ready, thinking about how they will go together.

1. Onion, celery and garlic. Saute all the vegetables until the onion turns transparent. Stir in the nuts.

2. Oats, mushrooms and cheese. Saute the mushrooms with the thyme in a covered pan, until their juices start to run. Stir in the oats and cheese.

3. Carrot and orange. Saute the carrots for 5 minutes, stirring. Add caraway seeds and carry on for a further 5 minutes. Stir in orange segments and jelly.

4. Aduki and swede. Dice swede and steam until soft. Mash with tahini and stir into beans.

5. Parsnips. Saute parsnips in butter until just soft, and stir in maple syrup.

Taste and season the stripes with salt and pepper. Once you have made the pastry, line a deep pie dish with two thirds, and layer up the filling: half the onion (1), half the oats and mushrooms (2), all the carrot (3), the swede (4), the rest of the onion and the rest of the mushrooms, and finally the parsnip (5). Seal in with a pastry top. Brush with egg, and bake at 170° for 1 hour. Cut with caution.

each piece as it is coated on a very well oiled baking sheet, turning once to coat both faces with oil. Bake at 160° for about 15 minutes, until golden brown. Keep warm.

Prepare the nasi goreng, and top with the tahu telur slices. Top each slice with a spoon of fresh mango sauce, and serve with the rest of the sauce separately.

NASI GORENG

Vary the vegetables according to what is seasonally and freshly available. Serves 6.

1 onion, chopped
2 carrots, cut into matchsticks
2 courgettes, in matchsticks
¼ small cauliflower, in bite sized florets
1 small head of broccoli, in florets
1 very small green and 1 very small red pepper, in strips
4 baby corn, split lengthwise
2 tablespoons sesame oil
1 teaspoon Chinese 5 spice
14 oz (400 gm) cooked brown basmati or long grain brown rice
1 tablespoon tamari

Stir fry the vegetables in the normal order, adding the spice with the carrots and onions. When everything is just tender, stir in the rice and tamari and continue stirring until all is heated through. Turn into a warmed dish and serve immediately.

TAHU TELUR WITH NASI GORENG & FRESH MANGO SAUCE

Literally means 'tofu-egg with fried rice', but the Indonesian words have a lovely ring! Tofu and its companion tempeh are made domestically in Indonesia, and used in a wide range of dishes. Tahu telur, usually served in a plaited banana leaf, is a typical Indonesian fast food. Serves 4.

1 block firm fresh tofu
1 quantity «Indonesian marinade»
4 tablespoons pineapple juice
wholewheat flour for dredging
3 egg yolks, beaten
sunflower oil for baking
«nasi goreng»
«fresh mango sauce»

Drain and press the tofu between clean cloths, under a heavy weight for at least an hour. Cut the block in half horizontally, and then cut each half into 4, making 8 thin slabs. Pour the marinade with the added pineapple juice into a shallow dish and lay the slabs in it. Leave to marinate several hours, or overnight, turning over from time to time.

Remove the tofu from the marinade and reserve the liquid for the sauce. Dredge each tofu slice with flour, dip in the beaten egg to coat completely, and again thoroughly dredge with flour. Lay

FIELD MUSHROOMS FILLED WITH SPINACH

Earthy and elegant at the same time. Serves 6.

12 large, flat mushrooms butter for greasing dish
1 clove garlic, crushed 2 oz (50 gm) butter or margarine 1 lb (450 gm) fresh spinach nutmeg, for grating
3 eggs, separated 5-6 oz (150-175 gm) wholewheat breadcrumbs

12 oz (350 gm) Sharpham Brie cheese

Butter a good looking dish. Remove stalks, and arrange mushrooms upside down on the dish bottom.

Briefly saute garlic and chopped mushroom stalks in butter. Add spinach and cook until just wilted. Add a generous grating of nutmeg.

Transfer the spinach to a food processor, and whizz for 10 seconds. Whisk egg whites to peaks. Beat yolks and crumbs into spinach. Fold in whites. Spoon onto mushrooms.

Put a slice of cheese on each filled mushroom. Bake at 150° for 30 minutes.

AUBERGINE, SWISS CHARD & MUSHROOM LATTICE PIE

Pecans and aubergines create a rich taste and texture, enhanced by the 'two vegetables-in-one', chard. Dairy free. Serves 6.

4 tablespoons olive oil 1 onion, sliced 3 aubergines, sliced pinch thyme 2 lb (1 kg) Swiss chard, washed and stalks set aside 2 lb (1 kg) tomatoes, chopped 2 tablespoons tomato paste 1 lb (450 gm) marron mushrooms, sliced
1 quantity «nut pastry» made with pecans egg for brushing

Heat oil and saute onion, aubergines, thyme and the sliced stalks of the chard (keep the leaves for later). Stir frequently until aubergine softens. Add tomatoes and paste. Cover and simmer for 5 minutes. Add mushrooms and chard leaves. Carry on cooking gently for another 15 minutes. Turn into a pie dish.

Roll out pastry and cut strips of a finger's width. Twist and put over filling to make a lattice pattern, and brush with egg. Bake at 170° for 35 minutes.

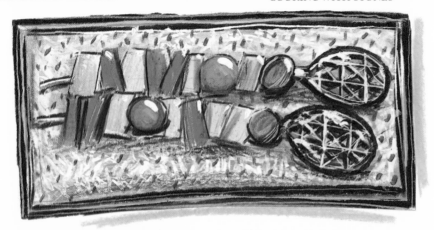

SATAY KEBABS WITH WILD RICE RISOTTO

These are splendid barbecued on a rack set above the coals. As an alternative to satay, you could fill some Polynesian skewers by substituting banana slices for the tomatoes, adding sliced mango or papaya and marinating the tofu in «Polynesian marinade». The quantities in this recipe will fill 10 large skewers, enough for 4-5 people.

1 block firm fresh tofu
1 quantity «Indonesian marinade»
2 teaspoons clear honey
1 quantity «wild rice risotto»
10 cherry tomatoes
10 whole button mushrooms
1 green and 1 red pepper, cut into ½ inch (2 cm) squares
½ a small pineapple, cut into slices and then into 20 cubes

Drain and press the tofu for at least 1 hour. Cut into 20 even sized cubes, and place in the marinade with the honey. Marinate several hours or overnight.

Prepare the risotto, and keep warm.

Assemble and prepare all the other ingredients. Remove the tofu and set it aside. Turn everything else in the marinade to coat. Now thread your kebab skewers, each with 2 cubes tofu, pepper squares of different colours, a cherry tomato, 2 pineapple cubes and a mushroom. Place the skewers across your barbecue rack and cook over hot coals, turning frequently and basting with the remains of the marinade. Alternatively, lay across a shallow baking dish and bake at 190° for about 20 minutes, basting occasionally, until the vegetables are just cooked. Arrange the hot kebabs on top of the wild rice risotto.

SWEET & SOUR ORIENTAL VEGETABLES

This is taking the stir fry a stage further by adding a poignant translucent sauce and lightly toasted nuts. Serves 6.

2 heaped tablespoons arrowroot
7 fl oz (200 ml) tomato juice
2 tablespoons tomato puree
3½ fl oz (100 ml) dry sherry
7 fl oz (200 ml) water
3 carrots, 3 courgettes and 2 celery sticks, sliced medium thick on the diagonal
1 onion, thinly sliced
1 cauliflower, in florets
1 red and 1 green pepper, sliced thinly
3 tablespoons sunflower oil
½ oz (15 gm) root ginger, grated
1 clove garlic, sliced
12 oz (350 gm) toasted cashews
1 lb (450 gm) mushrooms, whole and destalked

Start by making the sauce in a bowl, mixing the arrowroot with the tomato juice, and stirring in the other ingredients.

Saute the vegetables in the usual order in oil with the ginger and garlic. When onion turns transparent, pour over sauce and heat, stirring, until it thickens. Add a little extra tomato juice if needed.

Stir in the cashews and mushrooms. Check for seasoning. Serve with rice.

FLORENTINE STUFFED ALMOND ROAST WITH FRESH BASIL SAUCE

Celebrate Bastille Day, St Jean Baptiste day, or even someone's birthday with this wonderful midsummer roast. Never, ever, use frozen spinach for this recipe! Serves 6-8.

3 onions, finely chopped
2 tablespoons sunflower oil
18 oz (500 gm) mushrooms, thinly sliced
9 oz (250 gm) whole almonds, roughly chopped
4 oz (100 gm) ground almonds
4 oz (100 gm) wheatgerm
12 oz (350 gm) carrots, grated
2 tablespoons vegetable stock concentrate
4 eggs, beaten

18 oz (500 gm) spinach, weighed after large stalks removed
2 oz (50 gm) margarine
1 whole nutmeg, grated

whole almonds for decoration

Saute the onions in a little oil, gently, for 5 minutes. Add the mushrooms and continue gently cooking and stirring for 5 more minutes. Take off heat and stir in all the almonds, the wheatgerm, the carrot and the stock concentrate. Season to taste and bind with the beaten egg. Set aside.

Wash and spin dry the spinach and saute gently in the margarine with the nutmeg, until wilted. Finely chop or puree in your processor.

Now assemble the roast. Press half the mushroom-almond mixture into a well greased ovenproof dish. Spread the spinach puree on top. Cover with the remaining mushroom-almond mix.

Decorate with almonds. Bake at 180° for 45 minutes to 1 hour, until firm. Serve with «fresh basil sauce» and sauteed tiny new potatoes.

WILD RICE RISOTTO

Serves 6.

1 small onion, finely chopped
2 tablespoons sunflower oil
13 oz (375 gm) cooked brown basmati or long grain brown rice
2½ oz (75 gm) cooked wild rice
1 tablespoon tamari
3 tablespoons toasted flaked almonds
handful chopped fresh parsley

Saute the onion in the oil until transparent. Stir in the rice and the tamari, and keep stirring until all is hot. Stir in the almonds and parsley. Take off the heat and turn into a warm dish ready to serve.

BYZANTINE STUFFED PEPPERS

Mediterranean peppers with a jewelled interior. Serves 6.

6 roomy peppers (2 each red, green and yellow)
2 tablespoons sunflower oil
1 onion, chopped
1 fat garlic clove, crushed
5 small carrots, sliced
½ teaspoon oregano
3 sprigs fresh mint, chopped
3 sprigs fresh coriander, chopped
5 oz (150 gm) sultanas, soaked in ¼ pint
(150 ml) white wine

5 oz (150 gm) walnuts, ground
8 oz (225 gm) cooked rice
6 oz (175 gm) cooked wild rice
olive oil and white wine for baking

Slice off tops of peppers and remove the seeds and pith. Keep the tops.

Saute onion, garlic and carrots in oil with oregano. Add mint and coriander, and the wine and sultanas.

Remove from heat, and stir in nuts, rices and seasonings. Press mix into the pepper shells, stand them up in a tray or dish, and replace the lids. Drizzle over oil and enough wine to cover the bottom of the dish. Bake at 170° for 45 minutes, covered in foil.

SUNSET SHEPHERD'S PIE

This is the simple, comforting type of dish that can be waiting to go into the oven when you come back from a walk on the Ridgeway. Serves 6.

1 onion, sliced
4 carrots, sliced
1 red and 1 yellow pepper, sliced
1 aubergine, diced
4 tablespoons sunflower oil
1 lb (450 gm) cooked beans (eg aduki or
mung) or lentils
sprig rosemary
handful parsley, chopped

3 lb (1400 gm) mashed potato
4 oz (100 gm) margarine
12 oz (350 gm) Red Leicester cheese, grated
3 tablespoons tomato paste
8 tomatoes, sliced

Saute vegetables in oil. When aubergine softens, add beans and herbs. Add seasoning.

Prepare topping by mixing well together the mashed potato and other ingredients, and seasoning to taste.

Transfer pie filling to baking dish. Top with sliced tomatoes, then the cheese and potato mix. Bake at 180° for 60 minutes.

THANKSGIVING ROAST

First served as the centrepiece of the final lunch menu of our 1987 season, this roast was enjoyed by 70 hungry Cambridge archaeologists and countless regular and new customers besides. Complicated but worth the effort! Serves 6.

4 parsnips, sliced
2 oz (50 gm) margarine or butter
1 giant onion, finely chopped
2 sticks celery, finely sliced
4 large cloves garlic, crushed
2 tablespoons sunflower oil
9 oz (250 gm) mushrooms, chopped
4 tablespoons white wine
4½ oz (125 gm) toasted cashews, roughly chopped
5 oz (150 gm) toasted cashews, ground
4 oz (100 gm) wheatgerm
2 carrots, grated
a few sprigs of chopped fresh sage (or 2 teaspoons dried sage)
1 tablespoon dried thyme
zest of 1 large orange
½ nutmeg, grated
2 tablespoons tamari
salt and pepper
5 eggs, beaten

Melt the butter or margarine, add the parsnips and stir to coat. Add a splash of water, cover tightly and cook on low heat for about 10 minutes, until tender. Take off heat, mash and set aside.

Saute the onion, celery and garlic in oil until the onion is transparent. Add the mushrooms and wine and stir until the wine has evaporated. Remove from heat, and turn into a large bowl.

Stir in the cashews, the wheatgerm, carrots, herbs and seasonings. Add the mashed parsnips and stir until everything is thoroughly mixed. Bind with the beaten eggs and check the seasonings.

Layer half of this mixture in a well oiled baking dish, and prepare the filling.

1 small onion, finely chopped
2 cloves garlic, crushed
knob of butter or margarine
11 oz (300 gm) marron mushrooms, thinly sliced
4 tablespoons white wine
7 oz (200 gm) Swiss chard or spinach leaves, chopped
knob of butter or margarine
lemon slices and extra Swiss chard for decoration

Saute the onion and garlic in the butter for 5 minutes. Stir in the marrons and the wine, and stir until the wine evaporates. Set aside.

In another pan, saute the chopped leaves quickly for about 30 seconds, until just wilted. Remove from heat and chop very finely, or puree, in your food processor. Stir the puree into the marron mixture and season with lemon juice.

Spread this filling over the first roast layer and top with the rest of the parsnip-cashew mixture. Decorate with thinly sliced marrons. Cover with foil and bake at 180° for 1 hour. Remove the foil, and complete the decoration with lemon slices and finely chopped Swiss chard leaves. Serve with «mushroom-white wine sauce», or «redcurrant-orange sauce» and lightly steamed seasonal vegetables.

PUDDINGS

Illustrations by Sally Renwick

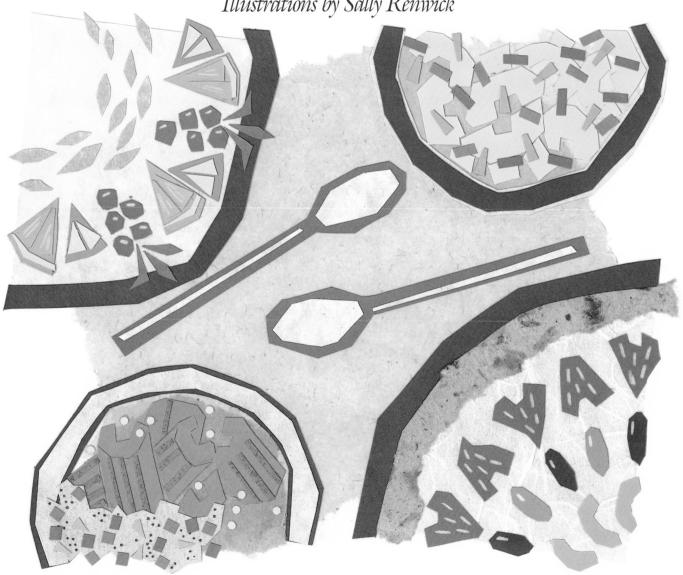

For an occasion: or for no reason at all, just because they look so good you can't resist them!

Aside from the sumptuous and colourful fruit salad with seasonal features such as blueberries, white currants or loganberries, the fruit pie is a perennial favourite on our counter. Full of the flavours of spice and citrus rind, it is served with a jugful of Guernsey cream.

Trifle, and similar sponge, fruit and cream combinations, have a long tradition, often associated with family high teas and parties. Whipping the cream with natural yogurt gives a rich yet lighter texture. Plain or flavoured wholewheat sponges absorb fruit juices, wines and liqueurs with less tendency to collapse than refined flour sponges.

A well finished pudding is most appealing. Make glazed pastry leaves and other shapes of your imagining for pies, and scatter over sesame seeds or demerara sugar. For the cold desserts, look to the garden for rose petals, nasturtiums, marigolds and geraniums. Toasted nuts, grated carob bar and fresh fruits look good too: just indulge your fancy!

TIPSY PUDDING

A light, fruity dessert with a delicious muscatel flavour of elderflowers.

1 lb (450 gm) lemon cake, or similar sponge
¼ pint (150 ml) elderflower wine
nectarines, peaches and pears, sliced
strawberries
blackberries
grapes, halved and de-pipped

9 fl oz (250 ml) whipping cream
4 fl oz (100 ml) natural yogurt
1 tablespoon clear honey
elder, borage, nasturtium or pansy flowers

Place broken sponge cake in an attractive dish. Pour over wine to moisten well. Next a layer of sliced fruits, just one or a combination.

Whip together cream, yogurt and honey to a soft, dropping consistency, and pour over the fruit. Decorate with more fruit and flowers. Chill briefly.

RHUBARB, ORANGE & GINGER CRUMBLE

Vary the fruits: **plums, damsons, greengages, apple and quince, blackberry and banana can all make wonderful crumbles. Oats, nuts and seeds create a topping full of flavour and crunch without heaviness.**

1 lb (450 gm) rhubarb, trimmed and washed
3 tablespoons orange juice
6 oz (175 gm) light muscovado sugar
¼ teaspoon ground ginger
3 oranges, peeled of skin and pith

4 oz (100 gm) jumbo oats
4 oz (100 gm) porridge oats
1 oz (25 gm) sesame seeds
2 oz (50 gm) pecan nuts, chopped
4 oz (100 gm) light muscovado sugar
6 oz (175 gm) margarine

Place rhubarb and orange juice in pan with sugar and ginger. Cook covered, until fruit begins to soften. Halve and slice oranges, and combine with rhubarb. Place in oven-proof serving dish.

To make topping, combine remaining dry ingredients in a roomy bowl and rub in margarine. Gently spread crumble over fruit. Bake at 150° for 30 minutes. Serve hot with fresh Guernsey cream or real custard (see «Stones trifle»).

FRUIT & OAT TART

A lighter crust for a glowing fruit filling sweetened with honeyed cream cheese.

8 oz (225 gm) butter
8 tablespoons clear honey
2 tablespoons light muscovado sugar
1 lb (450 gm) rolled oats
8 oz (225 gm) cream cheese
1 tablespoon tahini
1 tablespoon clear honey
all or any of these fruits:
green and black grapes, halved
nectarines, sliced
strawberries
red or white currants
tangerines
3 tablespoons redcurrant jelly
dash of white wine
strip or 2 of lemon rind

Start by making the oat base. Melt butter, honey and sugar together over a gentle heat. Simmer for 5 minutes. Pour onto oats in a bowl, mix well and press into a shallow, ovenproof flan dish. Bake at 150° for 30 minutes, until firm and turning golden. Allow to cool.

Beat together the cream cheese, honey and tahini and spread over the oat lined dish. Arrange your choice of fruits over the cream cheese.

Make a glaze by melting the redcurrant jelly with the wine and rind. Simmer to a syrup. Brush carefully over the fruit while warm.

STONES TRIFLE

Not just a mere trifle ...

1 plain or citrus «sponge cake»
2 tablespoons jam
1 banana, sliced
2 oranges, peeled and sliced
2 red and 2 green apples, cored and sliced
4 oz (100 gm) mixed green and black grapes, de-seeded
¼ pint (150 ml) orange juice
¼ pint (150 ml) sherry

3 eggs
3 egg yolks
2 heaped tablespoons arrowroot
1 teaspoon vanilla essence
1½ pints (850 ml) creamy milk
4 oz (100 gm) light muscovado sugar
¼ pint (150 ml) natural yogurt
¼ pint (150 ml) double cream
1 tablespoon clear honey
large handful toasted almonds, roughly chopped
extra grapes for decoration

Split the sponge and spread with jam or sponge cream. Cut into neat, but not too small pieces. Arrange the fruit pieces on the base and sides of a glass bowl, and fill with the sponge. Mix together the juice and sherry, and pour over. Leave to stand for ½ hour, or overnight in a cool place.

To make the custard, beat the egg yolks, arrowroot and whole eggs together with the vanilla essence. Gently heat the milk and sugar. When steam starts to rise, pour milk over eggs, whisking as you do so. Pour all back into pan and whisk over low heat until thickened to the consistency of double cream.

Pour custard over the sponge, and allow to cool. Meanwhile, whisk together yogurt, cream and honey. Spread this over cooled custard, then scatter nuts and arrange the halved grapes. Chill briefly before serving.

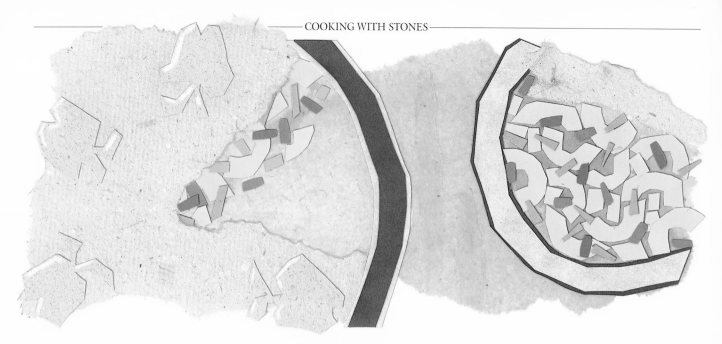

APPLE PIE

This impressive pie is shown off to its best made in an inch (2½ cm) deep, preferably cast iron flan dish: iron, because it conducts the heat better, through into the heart of the pie. The extra baking under foil is necessary to cook fully the great depth of fruit.

1 quantity «basic pastry»
½ teaspoon ground coriander
½ teaspoon ground cardamom
1 teaspoon ground cinnamon
2 tablespoons wholewheat flour
3 lb (1400 gm) Bramleys (weighed after coring), thinly sliced
zest of 2 oranges and 2 lemons
3 oz (75 gm) sultanas
9 oz (250 gm) demerara sugar
2 oz (50 gm) unsalted butter
3 tablespoons each orange and lemon juice
egg yolk and sugar for topping pastry

Line a well oiled and floured dish with slightly less than half the pastry.

Combine the spices with the flour in a small bowl (we call this our 'apple pie spice' in the restaurant).

Pack a third of the apple into the dish, and sprinkle with a third of the spice mixture, a third of the citrus zest, a third of the sultanas and a third of the sugar. Repeat this for two more layers.

Dot the butter over the top, and pour fruit juices over all. Cover with remaining pastry. Slash the top, and decorate with pastry leftovers (apple cutouts are useful if you have any splits in the pastry!). Brush with egg yolk, and sprinkle over sugar.

Bake at 150° for 35 minutes, or until golden brown. Then cover in foil, and bake a further 30-45 minutes, until the filling gives no resistance to a knife blade.

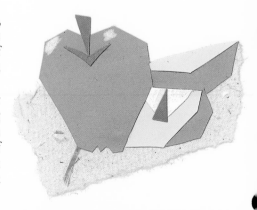

158

BREAD & BUTTER PUDDING

All a good pudding should be – creamy, soft, crunchy and comforting.

1 lb (450 gm) one or two day old wholewheat bread
6 oz (150 gm) unsalted farm butter
1 pint (550 ml) milk
7 fl oz (200 ml) single cream
4 egg yolks
2 oz (50 gm) light muscovado sugar
9 allspice berries, crushed
½ nutmeg, grated
grated rind of 1 lemon and 1 orange
8 oz (225 gm) lexia raisins
3 tablespoons demerara sugar

Slice bread fairly thinly; if using a large loaf, cut the slices into manageable pieces. Melt butter. Dip one side of the bread into the butter, and place in baking dish buttery side uppermost. Reserve remaining butter.

Heat milk. As it begins to simmer, remove from heat. Beat in cream, egg yolks, muscovado sugar and spices. Scatter fruit rind and raisins over bread. Pour in milk. Sprinkle demerara sugar over the bread and pour over remaining butter. Bake at 150° for 35 minutes, until bread is crisp and browned, and custard is just set.

CAROB & BANANA PUDDING

An invention of Julia's that, once tasted, can become an obsession.

1 lb (450 gm) «carob sponge»
4 heaped tablespoons «carob fudge filling»
milk to mix
1 tablespoon sherry or cognac
3 bananas
½ pint (300 ml) whipping cream
7 fl oz (200 ml) natural yogurt
3 tablespoons light muscovado sugar
carob drops to decorate

Crumble cake and place half in a handsome serving dish. Mix fudge filling with milk to make a thin carob sauce, and spoon half over cake. Slice over 2 bananas. Add sherry or cognac. Whip together the cream, yogurt and sugar to a soft, dropping consistency, and spoon half of this mix into the dish. Continue with the remaining cake, bananas and sauce (reserving a spoon or two for decoration). Top with rest of the cream and yogurt, swirl carob sauce over and scatter carob drops for a decorative finish.

BAKING

Illustrations by Tania Lomas

'Freshly baked scones, our own loganberry jam, and clotted cream from Cornwall! Also lots and lots of Stonesbaked cakes ... and much more!!' (Stones blackboard, 2.30-6.00 every day, April to late October).

As megaliths are our lunchtime showpiece, so the legendary cream tea is the focal point of the afternoon. Two golden brown, often still warm scones and a bowl each of our homemade jam and clotted cream, are served with a pot of tea or cup of coffee. Our scone cutters are worn thin and very sharp by the end of each season, having stamped out an estimated 20,000 scones!

All afternoon the fragrance of baking cakes and fruit scones wafts out across the stone circles. Earlier in the day (much earlier ...), the air is filled with the smell of delicious savoury cheese scones and newly baked bread. In this selection of our most popular baking recipes, we present you with the opportunity to recreate some of those magic aromas.

PIZZA BASE

This recipe will make enough dough for one pizza of the size we prepare at Stones. Our trays are about a foot (30cm) square. If your trays are smaller, left over dough makes super bread rolls!

8 fl oz (250 ml) water, straight from the hot tap
1 tablespoon dried yeast
1 tablespoon honey
about 1 lb (450 gm) wholewheat flour
1 teaspoon salt
3 tablespoons olive oil
extra olive oil for coating
1 small egg, beaten

Assemble the first three ingredients in a large bowl, and leave for about 5 minutes, until frothy.

Add 4 oz (100 gm) of flour, the salt and oil. Beat this mixture 100 times by hand, or for 3 minutes if using a machine with a dough hook. Gradually add more flour, beating all the time, until the mixture just loses its stickiness. Turn onto a lightly floured surface, and knead until springy. Lightly oil a clean bowl, and drop in the dough, turning it to coat all over with the oil. Put in a warm place to rise for about an hour, or until double in bulk.

Punch it down, and turn out once again onto a lightly floured surface. Roll out to fit your pizza tray. Brush the tray with oil and cover with the dough. If your tray does not already have a small lip, pinch up the dough to form one. Brush with beaten egg to seal the base (this stops the sauce soaking in and making the dough soggy). Bake at 200° for 7-10 minutes, until lightly browned and a bit puffy.

BREAD

Bread is ... bread. Of everything we make at Stones, our bread is perhaps the single thing that provokes most comment and interest. Our local paper ('The Wiltshire Gazette') once carried a story headed 'Hilary's bread is worth long trip', about an Edinburgh couple on holiday, who had made a substantial detour on their return journey for more bread.

The secrets of our bread, of any good bread, are simple but crucial: good flours, yeast and a feel in the baker for the magic of dough. In our modern world, the smell of traditional bread fresh from the oven is really special. Did you know that the vast bulk of 'bread' sold and consumed in this country is not made with yeast at all? Commercial bakeries make extensive use of premixes (akin to concretes or wallpaper pastes) to which the master baker adds water, and lets the chemicals do the rest.

So, here is our bread recipe. We use three different flours, all milled in Wiltshire. Wholewheat flour we buy (by the tonne!) from Rushall Farms, who produce a wonderful organic, stone ground wheat flour. 'Stone-white' is a brand name of Doves Farm. It refers to a strong (ie unbleached) white flour, and, uniquely, is also stone ground. Finally, 'Malthouse', another Doves Farm product, is a blend of wheat and rye malted flours and grains. There are several branded flours of this type on the market, of which the best known –

because most heavily marketed – is probably 'Granary' (Rank Hovis Macdougall's). As with the other flours, you should seek out your nearest mill and see if they can help you. Much of the character of bread comes from the distinctiveness of the flours employed. This is our bread: you must now make yours.

Makes about 15 rolls.

3 tablespons set honey (or 5-6 of clear honey) *3 tablespoons dried yeast* *1 pint (550 ml) hand hot water*
5 oz (150 gm) Stone-white *5 oz (150 gm) Malthouse* *2 tablespoons salt* *1 tablespoon carob flour* *5 tablespoons sunflower oil*
5 oz (150 gm) Malthouse *15-18 oz (425-500 gm) Rushall flour*
sunflower oil for proving

Put the honey, yeast and hot water into a large, round bowl and leave to froth (about 5 minutes).

Add the next 5 ingredients and beat 100 times.

Beat in the extra 5 oz (150 gm) of Malthouse, then gradually add the Rushall, beating and working with your hands as the mixture gets stiffer. When the dough is no longer sticky, but not dry, turn onto a lightly floured board and knead until smooth, satiny and bouncy.

Liberally oil a large bowl and introduce the dough. Turn the dough over and over until well coated with the oil. Put in a warm place and leave to rise (prove) until double in bulk (about 1 hour). Now, preheat your oven to 160°. Punch the dough down (this is very satisfying!) and mould into about 15 slightly smaller than tennis sized balls. Arrange the rolls (no more than 9 to a 1 foot/30 cm square tray, covered in baking parchment) and leave for 10 minutes in the warm place. Then cook the rolls in your preheated oven for about 20 minutes, or until they sound hollow when tapped on the bottom.

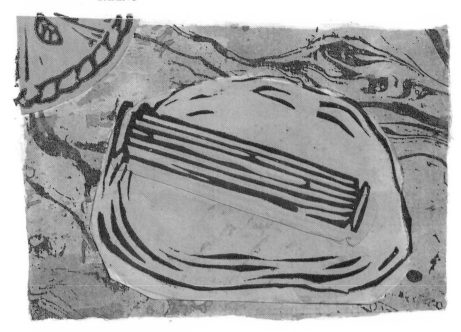

BASIC PASTRY

Lots of different people have to make pastry at Stones. Some find it difficult to handle a mixture made entirely with wholewheat flour. We therefore use this recipe for most of our pastry needs. As with the «bread», we use flours from Rushall and Doves Farms. But do try using all wholewheat: if you have good pastry hands, your pastry will be truly delicious!

8 oz (225 gm) margarine, frozen *8 oz (225 gm) wholewheat flour* *8 oz (225 gm) strong white flour*
1 egg *about ¼ pint (150 ml) cold water* *pinch salt*

Chop frozen margarine with strong knife, and place in food processor. Add flours and blend until resembling crumbs. Tip into a bowl.

Add egg, salt and water. Mix gently to form pastry.

SPONGE CAKE

We always (at least, at the start of each day ...) have five different filled sponge cakes on our counter. Each seems to be as popular as the other, whether it's carrot, carob fudge, plain (with clotted cream and soft fruit), lemon or orange. The basic sponge recipe that follows is for orange cake. You can substitute lemon, or omit the orange for a plain cake.

8 oz (225 gm) margarine
8 oz (225 gm) light muscovado sugar
8 oz (225 gm) wholewheat flour
4 eggs
½ tablespoon baking powder
zest and juice of 2 oranges

Cream the margarine and sugar together until smooth. Then add the eggs, one at a time, with a little of the measured flour. Mix baking powder with the rest of the flour, and add to the mixture. Zest the oranges, and mix the peel well in. Squeeze the fruits, and add 2 tablespoons of the juice. If the mix is too wet, add a litle extra flour. Spoon into a greased 8 inch (20 cm) diameter cake tin. Bake at 160° for about 40 minutes, until the cake is departing from the sides of the tin. Remove, and cool on a wire rack.

If you have made a plain sponge, all that remains is to cut it open and fill (and top) with clotted cream and soft fruit or jam. A citrus sponge, however, demands its own special cream.

166

ORANGE OR LEMON SPONGE CREAM

4 oz (100 gm) butter
4 oz (100 gm) light muscovado sugar
zest of 1 orange or 1 lemon
3 tablespoons orange or lemon juice
broken walnuts or flaked almonds to decorate

Beat butter and sugar together, then add zest and juice.

Cut open the sponge, and spread half of this filling on both faces before re-assembling the cake. That way, it will hold together better when you cut it.

After you have filled the cake, spread the rest of the cream on the top. It is easier to cut the cake now (into 10 wedges), then decorate with a scatter of nuts. We put almonds on our lemon cake, and walnuts on the orange. The main determinants of colour are the sugar and flour, so the almonds and walnuts help us tell which is which!

COCONUT CASTLES

Makes 10 castles. Save the egg yolks for «mayonnaise» or another purpose!

8 egg whites
12 oz (350 gm) light muscovado sugar
24 oz (675 gm) desiccated coconut
2 teaspoons vanilla essence
5 uncoloured glazed cherries, halved

Whisk egg whites until stiff. Add half the sugar and half the coconut, and the vanilla essence. Gently fold in the rest of the sugar and coconut. Mould into castles using a small cup (we use a half cup measure), dipping the cup into hot water before each moulding. Place the castles onto a baking sheet lined with baking parchment, and cook at 160° for 20 minutes, or until set and golden brown. Leave alone until completely cold, then decorate with the cherries.

SESAME CRACKERS

Makes about 15.

12 oz (350 gm) wholewheat flour
3 oz (75 gm) soya flour
½ teaspoon salt
4 oz (100 gm) toasted sesame seeds
¼ pint (150 ml) sunflower oil
about ¼ pint (150 ml) water

Thoroughly mix all the ingredients, except the water, in a large bowl. Gradually add the water until a rollable but not sticky dough is formed. Roll out thinly on a board dusted with flour and sesame seeds, and cut out with a 2 inch (5 cm) cutter. Bake at 160° for about 10 minutes, until firm. Do not brown, or they will taste bitter.

167

CAROB SPONGE

8 oz (225 gm) light muscovado sugar
8 oz (225 gm) margarine
4 eggs
2½ oz (75 gm) wholewheat flour
2½ oz (75 gm) ground almonds
2½ oz (75 gm) carob powder
½ tablespoon baking powder
½ teaspoon vanilla essence
¼ teaspoon almond essence
1 quantity «carob fudge cream»
apricot jam
pecan nuts to decorate

Cream together the sugar and the margarine. Add the eggs, one at a time, with a little flour. Mix in the rest of the dry ingredients, then drop in the essences. Spoon into a greased 8 inch (20 cm) diameter cake tin. Bake at 160° for 40-45 minutes or more, until the cake is coming away from the sides of the tin. Remove, and cool on a wire rack.

This rich sponge is made into a luxurious treat with lavish applications of «carob fudge cream». First split the cake and spread with apricot jam, then spread on half the carob cream, reserving the rest for the top. Finally, decorate the top of your cake with pecan nuts (after cutting into 10).

CARROT CAKE

A rich textured cake that we like to serve filled and topped with cream cheese, cut into 10 sumptuous slices.

10 oz (275 gm) wholewheat flour
1 tablespoon baking powder
1 teaspoon ground ginger
½ tablespoon coriander
½ teaspoon allspice
½ teaspoon cinnamon
9 fl oz (250 ml) sunflower oil
10 oz (275 gm) light muscovado sugar
4 eggs
12 oz (350 gm) carrot, grated
3 oz (75 gm) desiccated coconut
8 oz (225 gm) cream cheese
lots of black and green grapes to decorate, halved

Mix the flour with the baking powder and spices. In a large bowl, mix together the oil and the sugar. Add the eggs, one at a time, each with a little of the flour. Beat well after each addition. Stir in the carrot and the coconut. Fold in the dry ingredients. Turn the mixture into a well greased cake tin and bake at 160° for about 45 minutes, until a thin bladed knife comes out clean. Remove and cool on a wire rack.

When cold, split and spread both halves with cream cheese, reserving half for the top. Cut the entire cake into 10 wedges, and then decorate with the grapes.

CAROB FUDGE CREAM

3 oz (75 gm) butter
1 egg
2 oz (50 gm) carob powder
3-5 oz (75-150 gm) light muscovado sugar
¾ teaspoon instant coffee powder
¾ teaspoon vanilla essence
pinch salt
1 heaped tablespoon clotted cream

Beat together butter, egg and carob flour, then add other dry ingredients. Complete by beating in the clotted cream.

SHORTBREAD

Only butter will do for this recipe. Do not attempt with margarine!

8 oz (225 gm) butter
12 oz (350 gm) wholewheat flour
4 oz (100 gm) light muscovado sugar

Rub butter into flour, and stir in sugar. Work together to form a dough. Fill (the mixture will not rise) a shallow tin 7 inches (18 cm) in diameter, and prick the surface with a fork. Bake at 150°.

Cut into 8 pieces while still hot in the tin, and leave there to cool.

LEMON FINGERS

Cuts into 14-16 long fingers.

8 oz (225 gm) margarine
8 oz (225 gm) light muscovado sugar
4 eggs
8 oz (225 gm) wholewheat flour
1 tablespoon baking powder
zest of 2 lemons

2 oz (50 gm) light muscovado sugar
juice of 3 lemons

Cream together the margarine and sugar. Add the eggs, one at a time, each with a little flour to prevent curdling. Fold in the rest of the flour with the baking powder and lemon zest. Bake at 160° in a tray lined with baking parchment, until firm and golden. Leave to cool in the tin.

Make a syrup by melting the sugar with the lemon juice. Stab the sponge all over with a fork (almost to the bottom), and pour over the syrup. Leave to stand for at least 1 hour before cutting.

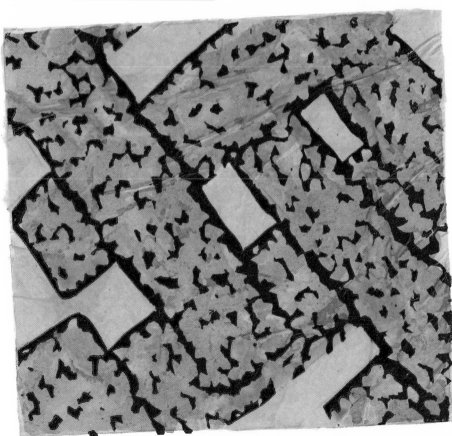

CHEESE SCONES

We make these scones at the same time as the bread, and the warm cheesy smell wafting from the basket on the counter is an essential part of the early morning for anyone serving! If you can obtain it, it really is worth using a good un-pasteurised cheddar. We buy three such cheeses (from Keen, Grant and Rainbow, all in Somerset), and the truly discerning customer would be able to distinguish them (after consuming quite a few scones ...).

The scones are best eaten while still slightly warm, spread with a farm made unsalted butter. This recipe makes about 10-12.

1 lb (450 gm) wholewheat flour
2 tablespoons baking powder
¼ teaspoon chilli powder
1 teaspoon salt
4 oz (100 gm) frozen margarine, chopped
12 oz (350 gm) cheese, grated
2 eggs, beaten
milk to mix

egg for brushing
extra cheese for topping

Mix the dry ingredients in the bowl of your processor. Add the margarine and blend to breadcrumbs.

Transfer to a large bowl and stir in the cheese, then the eggs and enough milk to mix into a firm dough, stiff but not sticky.

Roll out dough to 1½ inch (3½ cm) thickness, and cut out with a 2½ inch (6 cm) scone cutter. Brush each with egg and top with a generous pinch of grated cheese. Bake on parchment lined trays at 160° for 20 minutes.

STILTON & HERB MUFFINS

Delicious with «Boston baked beans», or on their own at breakfast time, hot from the oven, split and buttered. Experiment with different fresh and dried herbs and different cheeses. Makes 10-12 muffins.

9 oz (250 gm) wholewheat flour
1 heaped tablespoon baking powder
½ teaspoon salt
1 teaspoon dried thyme
1 tablespoon dried oregano
7 fl oz (200 ml) natural yogurt
7 fl oz (200 ml) milk
3 eggs
3 tablespoons sunflower oil
4 oz (225 gm) blue Stilton cheese, grated

Mix all the dry ingredients together in a large bowl.

In another bowl, mix the yogurt with the milk and beat in the eggs and the oil. Make a well in the dry ingredients and pour in the yogurt mix all at once. Stir to combine everything, then fold in the cheese. Spoon the mixture into a well oiled muffin pan, almost filling each cup. Bake at 175° for 25 minutes, or until well risen and golden brown.

DATE SLICES

Known at Stones as 'the world famous date slices', ever since a Texan came into the restaurant for his first visit (his Louisianna friend had recommended him to come) and exclaimed: 'There are those world famous date slices!' Makes about 20 slices or squares.

16 oz (450 gm) chopped dates
4 oz (100 gm) wholewheat flour
½ pint (300 ml) cold water
1 teaspoon vanilla essence
8 oz (225 gm) carob nuggets
12 oz (350 gm) margarine
12 oz (350 gm) wholewheat flour
12 oz (350 gm) jumbo oats
8 oz (225 gm) light muscovado sugar
1 tablespoon baking powder

Make the date mix by cooking all the ingredients over a gentle heat, stirring all the time to avoid sticking.

In a separate pan, melt the margarine then add the flour, oats and sugar. Spread half of this crumble mixture onto the bottom of a baking tray. Put the date mixture on top, then add the rest of the crumble. Bake at 150-160° for about 45 minutes, until just golden brown, but not set. The mixture sets as it cools.

Allow to cool completely in the tin, then cut into slices or squares with a sharp serrated knife.

171

BAKEWELL TART

½ quantity «basic pastry»
2 tablespoons homemade strawberry or raspberry jam
6 oz (175 gm) butter
3 oz (75 gm) light muscovado sugar
3 eggs
4oz (100 gm) ground almonds
3 oz (75 gm) wholewheat flour
1 teaspoon baking powder
½ teaspoon almond essence
a few drops of vanilla essence
flaked almonds for topping

Make the pastry, roll out and line a shallow tin 8½ inches (22 cm) in diameter. Spread the bottom thinly with jam.

Cream butter and sugar, then add eggs, one at a time, each with a little of the flour. Add ground almonds, the rest of the flour, baking powder and essences. Pour into the lined tin, making sure that the jam does not rise up around the edges (or the mix will not bind, and the pastry will fall off!). Sprinkle flaked almonds over the top. Bake at 160° for 25 minutes, or until firm and golden brown.

Allow to cool in tin, and remove to cut into 8 with a sharp knife.

FRUIT SCONES

Makes 10-12 scones, best eaten while still just warm with homemade jam and clotted cream.

1 lb (450 gm) wholewheat flour
2 tablespoons baking powder
1 level teaspoon salt
6 oz (175 gm) frozen margarine, chopped
1 oz (25 gm) demerara sugar
2 oz (50 gm) sultanas
2 eggs, beaten
milk to mix (about 4-5 fl oz/100-150 ml)
extra flour for kneading
egg for brushing

Put flour, baking powder and salt into the bowl of your food processor. Add the margarine and blend to breadcrumbs. Turn out into a bowl and stir in the sugar and sultanas.

Add the eggs and just enough milk to result in a soft but not sticky dough. Turn the mixture onto a floured surface and knead until it feels bouncy. Now, take a floured rolling pin and roll the scone dough to 1½ inches (3½ cm) thickness. Cut out with a 2½ inch (6 cm) fluted cutter. Arrange the scones, well spaced, on parchment lined sheets. Brush with beaten egg and bake at 160° for about 20 minutes or until just firm.

RICH ALMOND PASTRY

This pastry is perfect for a fresh fruit flan. It is quite difficult to handle, and not really suitable for pies or more complex constructions. But it's too yummy to worry much about problems like that!

1 lb (450 gm) wholewheat flour
4 oz (100 gm) ground almonds
½ teaspoon almond essence
4 oz (100 gm) light muscovado sugar
pinch salt
8 oz (225 gm) butter (preferably frozen), chopped
yolks of 4 eggs
ice cold water

Mix the first five ingredients in a food processor, add the butter and blend until the mixture looks like breadcrumbs.

Turn into a bowl, and stir in the egg yolks and just enough water to give a firm dough. Roll in cling film and chill for at least 1 hour.

On a well floured board with a well floured rolling pin, roll to fit large or individual flan dishes. Persevere: the patches won't show!

DIGESTIVE BISCUITS

Makes about 15.

12 oz (350 gm) wholewheat flour
½ teaspoon salt
5 oz (150 gm) margarine
2 oz (50 gm) demerara sugar
about 4 teaspoons water

Rub the margarine into the flour and salt mixture. Stir in the sugar and add just enough water to bind the mixture. Roll thinly on a lightly floured board, and cut out with a 2 inch (5 cm) cutter. Bake at 160° for about 10 minutes, until just turning golden. Do not brown.

NUT PASTRY

4 oz (100 gm) nuts
8 oz (225 gm) margarine, frozen
8 oz (225 gm) wholewheat flour
8 oz (225 gm) strong white flour
1 egg
about ¼ pint (150 ml) cold water
pinch salt

Place nuts in processor, and reduce to a fine crumb texture. Remove to a bowl.

Chop margarine and process with flours.

Add margarine and flours to nuts with salt, egg and water. Combine to form pastry.

FRUIT & NUT BARS

Makes about 8 bars. These bars, extremely popular in the restaurant, have no sugar, no gluten, no eggs and no dairy products. More often than not, the serving plate has no bars!

1 lb (450 gm) dried apricots
4 oz (100 gm) dried apple rings
4 oz (100 gm) dried peaches
8 oz (225 gm) lexia raisins
4 oz (100 gm) peanuts
4 oz (100 gm) almonds
4 oz (100 gm) broken brazil nuts
4 oz (100 gm) desiccated coconut
3 tablespoons sunflower oil
1 teaspoon almond essence
6 tablespoons apple concentrate
4 oz (100 gm) soya flour
4 oz (100 gm) brown rice flour

Coarsely chop the apricots, apple and peaches, and simmer, with the lexias, in just enough water to cover for 1-1½ hours, until all are soft. Meanwhile chop the nuts. Cool the fruit and tip into a large bowl. Stir in all the other ingredients and mix well by hand. Put into a baking tin lined with parchment, and bake at 170° for about 1 hour, until just firm. Cover with foil if it shows signs of catching. Cool in the tin, and cut into bars when cold (a very sharp serrated knife is best for this).

GINGERBREAD PEOPLE

Will make about 20, depending on the size of your cutter(s).

12 oz (350 gm) wholewheat flour
1 tablespoon baking powder
2 teaspoons ground ginger
4 oz (100 gm) margarine
6 oz (175 gm) demerara sugar
3 tablespoons molasses
1 egg, beaten
currants to dress

Mix the flour, baking powder and ginger together and rub in the margarine. Stir in the sugar and molasses. Stir in the beaten egg and knead the mixture well. Roll out on a well floured board to two tenths of an inch (5 mm) thick. Cut out your people with gingerbread cutters and decorate with currants first dipped in water (they stick better this way!). Bake at 160° for 7-10 minutes on parchment lined sheets. Be careful not to over-tan them: they do not harden up until they have cooled.

BANANA LOAF

This recipe makes one 2 lb (900 gm) loaf. Sliced and buttered, it makes a delicious accompaniment to a cup of tea or coffee. The loaf can be frozen and matured for 2-3 months, when its flavour will deepen and the texture moisten.

12 oz (350 gm) wholewheat flour
½ teaspoon salt
2 teaspoons baking powder
1½ teaspoons cinnamon
7 oz (200 gm) light muscovado sugar
4 oz (100 gm) margarine, melted
3 eggs
4 large bananas, thoroughly mashed
6 oz (175 gm) sultanas

Mix the flour, salt, baking powder and cinnamon in a bowl. In another large bowl, combine the sugar with the melted margarine. Beat in the eggs separately, each with a little of the flour mix, into the sugar-margarine mixture. When all the eggs have been thoroughly incorporated, fold in the rest of the dry ingredients. Next, stir in the bananas. Finally, fold in the sultanas. Turn the entire mixture into a lined 2 lb (900 gm) loaf tin and bake at 160° for 50-60 minutes, or until a thin blade comes out clean.

CAROB CHIP COOKIES

Makes 8-10.

4 oz (100 gm) margarine
4 oz (100 gm) demerara sugar
1 teaspoon baking powder
9 oz (250 gm) wholewheat flour
1 oz (25 gm) ground almonds
1 egg, beaten
3 oz (75 gm) carob chips

Cream the margarine and sugar. Mix the baking powder with the flour and ground almonds. Beat the egg with a little of the flour mixture into the creamed margarine. Stir in the carob chips. Form the mixture into golf sized balls and put on parchment lined baking sheets. Space well, as the cookies spread during baking. Bake at 170° for 15-20 minutes.

INDEX

Illustrations by Alison Dexter

INDEX OF RECIPES

Many of our customers ask us for gluten free or vegan dishes, so we have identified such recipes here with a G or a V.

BAKING

MEGALITHS

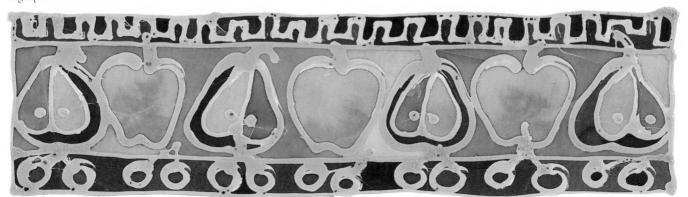

PORTABLE SAVOURIES

PUDDINGS

SALADS

SAUCES

STONESOUPS

INDEX OF INGREDIENTS

Perhaps you bought a wonderful cauliflower, a bunch of bright broccoli, or a perfect pound of mushrooms in the market? Or is your garden overflowing with runner beans or spinach? Maybe you have cooked lots of pulses or rice and are looking for ways to use them up? Or have you simply got the urge to cook something with cheese?

If your answer to any question like these is 'yes', this index will help you. It groups recipes by major ingredient, and is designed to channel your inspiration from your raw materials, through kitchen to table.

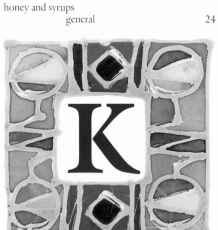

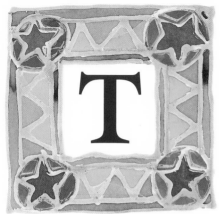